Memoirs of a Recovering Teacher

Memoirs of a Recovering Teacher

David Peterson
with
Peter Davidson

SWEET MEMORIES PUBLISHING

A Division of Sweet Memories, Inc.

sweetmemories@mchsi.com

If you purchased this book without a cover, you should be aware that this book is stolen property. It was reported "unsold and destroyed" to the publisher and neither the author nor the publisher has received any payment for this "stripped book."

This book contains reference to real stories about real people; however, people generally are not identified by their real names and in many cases, persons' roles, positions, or titles have been changed to protect the actual identity of the persons depicted in the stories. All of the events and stories in the book are a product of the author's remembrance and interpretation of these events, which might vary slightly from the actual events themselves.

Copyright © 2013 by David R. Peterson

All rights reserved. No part of this book may be used or reproduced in whole or part or transmitted in any form or by any means, electronic or mechanical, without permission from the publisher except for a reviewer who wishes to use brief quotations for a review in newspapers, magazines, or other form of broadcast. For information address Sweet Memories Publishing, Sweet Memories, Inc., P.O. Box 497, Arnolds Park, IA 51331-0497.

ISBN: 978-0-9762718-5-7
Library of Congress Control Number: 2012944153
First printing, July, 2013

Published by Sweet Memories Publishing, Sweet Memories, Inc.
P.O. Box 497, Arnolds Park, IA 51331-0497

PRINTED IN THE UNITED STATES OF AMERICA

10 9 8 7 6 5 4 3 2 1

Acknowledgments

Editor: Beterzone Wordright Services

Graphic Design: Debbie Wilson

Front and Back Cover Photos: David DeVary

eBook Design & Marketing: Jean Tennant

Readers: L. Louwagie, C. Marshall, B. Peterson, K. Schendel, N. Schendel, B. Schomaker

Dedications

To my wife, Bev, who has heard each of these stories dozens of times through the years and who, nevertheless, consented to read the manuscript to make sure that I told them accurately.

To each person who is the subject of one or more of the stories in this book, thanks. Your identity is safe with me. Since the events described in this book cover a time span of several decades and a significant geographic area, it is possible that several different people may have been involved in events similar to those described in the book. In other words, the story may not even be about you. But, if you want to identify yourself and take the credit, or blame, you're on your own.

To anyone who has ever been a student, be assured that, even though your teachers may have been perplexed by you at one time or another, they still cared for you and hoped for the best for you.

To anyone who has ever been a teacher, administrator, secretary, custodian, or other employee of any school or college, you'll probably recognize many of the occurrences presented here as similar to those that you have witnessed first-hand. Perhaps you'll want to share a few of your own stories with colleagues and friends.

To you, the reader, please be aware that these stories are presented not to embarrass or ridicule anyone involved, but are, instead, intended for your amusement and enjoyment. As for me, I sure enjoyed telling them.

David Peterson

Table of Contents

In Recovery...1

Choosing a Career.....................................3
   Inspired By Some Teacher?..........................4
      Country School.................................5
      Town School....................................7
      High School....................................8
   A Family Tradition?...............................15
   To Contribute To Society?.........................16
   My Real Reason For Becoming A Teacher.............17

Choosing a College Major..............................19

A College Stoodent....................................21
   Registering For Classes...........................22
   My Personal Faculty Advisor.......................23
   Just Trying To Have A Little Fun..................26
      Judy, Judy, Judy...............................26
   A Few More College Daze Stories...................29

Job Hunting...31
   A College Graduate – And Back To The Farm.........31

This Is Teaching? (Faculty In-Service)................35

Whoda Thunk It – A College Professor..................39
   Faculty Inservice, College Style..................39

Students..45
   Harold..45
   Investigative Reporters...........................49
   The Mass Cut......................................51
   Course Syllabus...................................54

    Class Attendance Policy 55
        Sammy the Sometime Student. 56
    Classroom Pranksters. 61
        Turning The Tables 64
    Student Demonstrations. 66
    Sue 'Em 70
    And Then, I Remembered What You Taught Me 73
    Quotable Quotes 75
    A Tender Side. 80

Tests And Grading 83
    Giving Exams. 84
    World-Class Cheaters. 85
        Leonard, The Amazing Accountant 85
        Cool Conrad 92
        A Way With Words. 94
    Mysterious Fall From Grace 95
    Begging For A Grade 98

Students: They're Almost. 105

The Faculty 107
    The Exhibition 108
    A Wedding To Remember 110
    Mathematical Wizardry 113
    The Halftime Speech. 114
    Steven Marcus Becker. 116
    "Bridges" 132
    "Lil Hitchhiker" 133
    Television Stars 134
    The Booksellers 135
    Signs 139
    The Poison Pen. 140

- Faculty Meetings 146
  - Elvis Was Here 147
  - And In This Corner, Weighing In At… 147
  - Faculty Lounge Under Attack 148
- The Great Debate 150
- That Leisurely Lifestyle 152

Administrators 155
- "Listen, People" 155
- The Book Club 158
- Voter Strategy 160
- The Petition 162
- Joining The Ranks 169

Moonlighting 171
- Life Insurance Sales 171
- Driver Training 173
- The Glass Man 177
- IGL Recording Company 179
- Real Estate Sales 180
- Real Estate Pre-License Course 183
- The Author 184
  - Shoebox Accounting 185
  - Writing Up A Storm 187
  - Meet Peter Davidson 189
- Peter Davidson's Writer's Seminars 191
- All Work And No Play… 192

Surviving 195
- Survival Techniques 195

The Decision 203

On The Road To Recovery 205

In Recovery

My friend, George, told me that when he was honorably discharged from the navy some years ago, they said that it would take two years of recovery to get back to normal for every year he had spent in the navy. I personally believe that this same formula applies to teachers who retire or leave the profession.

Since I was a teacher for thirty-eight years - four years in high school and thirty-four years at a community college, it will take seventy-six years before I am fully recovered. I retired from teaching at age 59 to pursue other interests such as writing this book; therefore, I will be 135 years old when I am fully recovered. To celebrate my return to being normal, I intend to throw one hell of a party. You're invited.

This book consists of true stories from my life as a teacher and of the people that I met along the way. The stories are about students, faculty, and administrators - and about survival. When you read some of the stories, you're apt to say to yourself, "He made that up - it *couldn't* be true." But it is.

After reading these stories, I trust that you will fully understand the aforementioned formula about two years of recovery that are needed for every year of teaching.

–*David R. Peterson*

Choosing a Career

Many of my colleagues in the teaching profession can pinpoint the exact moment when they decided to become a teacher, as though it were some kind of religious experience, and they can tell you precisely why they became a teacher. For some, it was their third grade teacher, Miss Snodgrass, or their high school English teacher, Mr. Whipple, who inspired them to follow in their footsteps. For others, it was to serve, to shape young minds, and to make a contribution to society. Still others chose teaching because both of their parents, their grandparents, and all of their uncles and aunts were teachers and it was their destiny to uphold the family tradition. I suspect others had been brilliant students and they decided to share their brilliance with lesser minds in a classroom setting.

During my thirty-eight year career as a teacher, I never stopped to analyze exactly why I became a teacher; it just more or less seemed to happen. When I decided to write this book, it appeared to me that it was finally time to answer that question for my own satisfaction and for you, too, so you can more fully understand some of the stories that I am about to tell you.

Inspired By Some Teacher?

So, was I inspired by some brilliant teacher that I had when I was a student? Well, I grew up on a farm in southwest Minnesota. For many years, prior to my entering school, farm kids attended country school through eighth grade and then went to town school for grades 9–12. When I was a child, though, farms were becoming larger which meant that there were fewer farm families and thus fewer farm kids for the country schools. The days of the one-room country schoolhouse were numbered.

It was obvious that the country school serving our rural township was on the brink of collapse because of declining enrollment. The teacher held only a two-year teaching certificate, which was grandfathered in and was permissible for teaching in a country school, but a four-year degree was required by the local school board in order for someone to teach in the town school. Thus, when her country school closed down, she would be out of a job. The country schoolteacher, therefore, took matters into her own hands to keep the school open as long as possible – she recruited students.

When I was barely four years old, the country schoolteacher paid a visit to my parents. She looked me over, asked me a couple of questions, sized me up, and pronounced me big enough, old enough, and smart enough to start school in the fall – none of which, by the way, were even close to being accurate. Since there was no kindergarten in country schools, I would go directly into first grade. My parents came from the old school where a teacher was respected and trusted and whatever the teacher said was accepted as the gospel. So, off to school it was.

Country School

There were three of us in the first grade and another five students in grades two through eight. Not a big enough student body to field a baseball team, but big enough to keep the doors open at least one or two more years.

The other students in the first grade were evenly divided between boys and girls – one of each. I had seen the girl somewhere before but had never laid eyes on the boy. I was duly impressed, though, when his dad dragged him into the schoolhouse by the ear as the boy was kicking and screaming. In the other hand, the one that wasn't holding onto the ear, the dad carried a sawed-off boat oar about three feet long with a crack in it. He handed the boat oar to the teacher and said, "Don't be afraid to use this on him if he gets out of line."

I felt terribly sorry for my new classmate, Delbert, and I could tell just by looking that the rest of the student body felt sorry for him also.

After just two days of school, however, I came to realize that Delbert's dad wasn't such a bad guy after all. Delbert was the meanest, sneakiest, lyingest, nastiest, cheatingest, most worthless little bastard I'd ever seen in my life. Every time the teacher turned her back, Delbert would pull the hair of the girl in our class or try to punch or kick me. And, he must have had a death wish because he also picked on the upperclassmen. By the end of the third day of school, the entire student body was praying for the teacher to bring out the boat oar and give Delbert what he deserved.

One day, in the middle of the second week of school, the teacher opened her lunchbox and found nothing but an apple core and some waxed paper that once held her sandwich. She came unglued. She accused Delbert, but he denied it. She went to get the boat oar to beat the truth out of him, but it was missing. As we learned later, Delbert had thrown it down into the pit in the outhouse several days before eating the teacher's lunch.

Not having the boat oar available to mete out a proper punishment to Delbert, the teacher imposed the next most horrible punishment that she could think of – she sat Delbert on a stool in the back corner of the room facing the wall and put the *Dunce Hat* on his head and ordered him to sit there for the remainder of the day. For the uninformed, the dunce hat was a cone-like hat that resembled a Halloween witch's hat that had the word, *DUNCE*, written on it in big letters. Any time a student did something dumb, or was naughty, the teacher would sit them in the corner and make them wear the dunce hat. I, of course, never had to wear the dunce hat, but most of the student body did at one time or the other.

From time to time, I ponder the chicken and egg theory as it pertained to Delbert – you know, which came first, the chicken or the egg? But in Delbert's case I wonder which came first – the boat oar or the nastiness? But, one thing is for certain, Delbert was the meanest, sneakiest, lyingest, nastiest, cheatingest, most worthless little bastard I've ever known.

When I was in second grade, there were only three students in the whole school and it folded after that year.

Town School

I entered town school in the third grade and made a huge discovery – the rest of the students in my class could read and print and they were starting to write in cursive. Apparently, although the country schoolteacher kept the doors open those extra two years, she had actually quit teaching the fall that I entered first grade. I built a birdhouse, I recall, and played a lot of games, but we didn't get into the academics. The third grade teacher assumed that there was a simple explanation to why I could not read or write – I was stupid.

My mother would not accept the teacher's assessment that a child of hers could not read or write because he was stupid and she hit upon the idea that maybe I had eyesight problems and needed glasses.

My mother took me to the doctor for an eye checkup. In our small rural town, there was only one doctor who did it all from physical exams to treating any and all ailments known or unknown to mankind. He was also the eye doctor and would even pull a tooth or perform surgery in an emergency.

The doctor sat me down in a chair and used a projector to put some letters up on the wall. They were X P R G K Z. "Can you read that?" he asked. I thought I was there for an eye exam, but the doctor had ambushed me with a reading exam – X P R G K Z – it was the damndest word I'd ever seen. "No," I admitted. I could not read the word. The doctor continued flashing other complicated words up on the wall, each one bigger in size than the previous one – words like T V Y W X, B L P Z, and Q Y P. Finally, he put something on the wall that I could read - a great big E - and I shouted out, "E."

The doctor confirmed what my mother had suspected. Perhaps I wasn't stupid – he wasn't sure - but I definitely needed glasses. And, that is how I came to wear the pair of pink plastic framed glasses that I am seen wearing in my third grade picture.

Now, in addition to not being able to read or write, I had another handicap to overcome – trying to see out of a pair of eyeglasses that made my eyes spin.

I had a lot of ground to make up in reading and writing, but with noontime tutoring from my older brother and nighttime tutoring from my mother, I finally caught up with most of them by the end of the third grade.

Except for that country schoolteacher, I recall that my elementary and junior high teachers were kind and competent, but I can't repeat any of their names. It is therefore safe to say, that none of them were the guiding light that led me into a teaching career.

High School

Ours was a small high school, with about thirty or thirty-five students in each grade. Therefore, there was one math teacher, one English teacher, one social science teacher, one science teacher, one business teacher, and one music teacher who taught all of the courses in their discipline for grades

9-12. I recall one particular trait or incident about each of these teachers.

The math teacher was also the football coach. He took mathematics seriously, was a good mathematician, and was a good math teacher. However, he took football about ten times more seriously than mathematics and considered any boy who didn't play football to be a wimp or a pussy. In his mind, even worse than a boy who didn't play football was a football player who also played in the school band.

Somehow, the band director had convinced the school Principal that each band member should be allowed to miss class for a half hour a week to go to the band room for a practice session. The practice schedule was on a rotating basis, so a band member would miss a different class each week, thus missing any particular class only once in a five-week cycle.

It drove the math teacher wild when any of his students left halfway through class to go to the band room for their practice session. But, when a football player left his class for a practice session, he went insane. I recall him staring at me with a red face and bulging eyes like I had given the coveted football playbook to our archrivals. Then with a sneer he would growl something through clenched teeth like, "Well, look at Mr. Rooty-Toot-Toot." Then he would stare straight at me, the traitor, for a full thirty seconds. Finally, he'd yell something like, "Go on, get the hell out of here – go play your damn horn." And he had a way of saying *horn* that made it the most despicable of all four-letter words. He'd finish off his tirade by slamming shut his math textbook and by standing there shaking his head from side to side, muttering to himself, while you whimpered out the door. And, you just knew that at football practice that day he'd be laying for you. And, if you got injured in practice or in a game, whether you had a broken leg, concussion, or anything in between, his response was always the same, "Be a man, work it out, get back in there."

No, this guy didn't inspire me to be a math teacher, he didn't inspire me to be a football coach, and he certainly didn't inspire me to become a music teacher. But he did teach me a valuable lesson about intimidation – compared to this guy, every person I've ever met in my life who tried to intimidate me has been, at best, a pussycat.

The English teacher was good at punctuation, spelling, and sentence structure and didn't like those who weren't. It was before the days that I developed an interest in writing, so I fell into the latter category. She had a shrill voice and when she got excited or started lecturing us about the immoral behavior of teenagers these days, her voice would raise an octave or two.

One Monday at the start of class, she chitchatted with us, real nice and pleasant about the past weekend. "Did you enjoy the nice weather?" "Did any of you see the new movie playing at the theater – *Cat On A Hot Tin Roof?*"

Rarely did I, or my best buddy, Richard, have the opportunity to volunteer an answer in class, but this time we did. We had gone to the movie and had been talking about it ever since. Our hands shot straight up and we waved frantically with big smiles on our faces.

One look at the scowl on her face was enough to tell us that she had laid a trap and that we had marched straight into it. As we were about to discover, *Cat On A Hot Tin Roof* was considered to be a racy and sexually explicit movie for the times and was extremely controversial.

"That is the most disgusting and evil movie that has ever been made," she began, looking straight at the two of us. "Anyone who went to that movie should be ashamed of themselves. That movie is corrupting the morals and values of people of all ages, etc. etc. etc…"

Richard and I both flunked English that grading period.

That was the last time that I ever volunteered anything in English class, or damn near any other class for that matter. My English teacher did not inspire me to become a teacher, but I did learn from her to be very suspicious when all of a sudden someone becomes super sweet and friendly.

The science teacher was a good guy. He taught general science, biology, chemistry, and physics and he knew them all. When you couple the fact that we were scientific bunglers with the additional fact that some in our class were a little mischievous, it must have been perplexing for him to deal with us. I can still recall him yelling at us two or three times a class period, *"This is going to come to a screeching halt!"* What a great line.

I wouldn't say that he inspired me to become a teacher, but he did show me that teachers can be honorable.

The social science teacher was also a good guy with a lot of charisma. His name was Corliss and he loved Hubert

Horatio Humphrey, who was at the time a U.S. senator from the state of Minnesota. His enthusiasm made history and social studies come alive and although I couldn't remember all of those dates and didn't share his enthusiasm for the subject matter, I think I saw for the first time that teaching could be fun.

The business teacher taught typing and bookkeeping, plus some secretarial courses. He, too, was a good guy. I didn't know it until the last week of my senior year in high school, but my taking one of his classes would unexpectedly help shape my entire professional life and profoundly affect my personal life. But, more on that later.

The music teacher/band director was a roly-poly guy with a large girth, weak chin, and huge smile. At first glimpse, you'd dismiss him as being a cream puff, but he had the balls to stand up to the football coach in creating half-hour practice sessions for band members during academic class periods, including math class, and he won. He was a good band director and created a good concert band and an acceptable marching band, given the material that he had to work with.

The band director had this obsession with practicing, expecting each of us in the band to practice, practice, practice every day. He even hung this chart on the wall of the band room that listed everyone's name and the amount of practice time that they logged at home, measured by a line graph with an inch on the graph representing one hour of practice time. By the end of the grading period, some of them had lines on the graph over three feet long and he had to add an extra piece of tag board to the graph.

My buddy, Richard, played the tuba and had a half-inch line on the graph. I was the only one in the band who had a line on the graph that didn't even leave home – like zero hours of practice. Perhaps I was the least interested and worst member of the band, but I prefer to think of myself as being the most honest member of the band. I believe that I am the only person in the history of the high school who ever received an "F" in band.

Strange as it might seem, I liked the band director, and he liked me. The "F" wasn't anything personal, he told me, it's just that I didn't practice like I was expected to.

It might appear that I didn't have the music in me, but I did. It's just that it was hard to get my fingers to play show tunes, waltzes, and marches when my heart and soul were wrapped around Rock 'N' Roll.

When it came to decision time about my plans after high school graduation, the band director was the one person in the school system who most strongly suggested that I attend college and who convinced my parents that I could do it, if I put my mind to it. He taught me, among other things, that even if you don't agree with someone on everything, you can still have faith in them and can still support them and hope for the best for them.

The high school Principal also doubled as the school counselor, since our school was too small to afford a real counselor. His role as counselor was limited to three things: conducting an I.Q. test, conducting an aptitude test, and meeting with the student and his or her parents once to discuss the results of those two tests and to make a recommendation about what the student should do after high school graduation.

The aptitude test, which purported to show which occupations or professions would be a good match for you, provided me with no help whatsoever in choosing a career. My highest match was to be an undertaker and my lowest was to be a minister. I already knew that I didn't want to be a minister and when the aptitude test said that I should devote my life to working with the dead, I considered the entire test to be flawed and didn't even consider what it had chosen for me as second, third, and fourth choices for a career.

When it came to discussing the results of the I.Q. test, the Principal turned counselor dropped a bombshell. Basically, he said that I wasn't as dumb as I appeared. He could have stopped there, but then he went on to explain to my parents all of the things that I could have and should have accomplished academically in high school that I didn't. He always had a knack for doing that - patting you on the back with one hand and stabbing you with the other.

His final recommendation was that I had the ability to accomplish a lot of things in life, but based on my high school performance it would probably be a waste of my time and of my parent's money to send me to college. Again, patting and stabbing at the same time.

Obviously, his words did not inspire me to enter the education field, or any field, for that matter.

So, was I inspired to become a teacher by one of my own teachers? As you can see from the preceding revelations, there were a couple of positives, a couple of negatives, and a couple of neutrals – pretty much a draw.

Years later, after I had accomplished a few things that are chronicled in this book, my mother would occasionally look at me with a twinkle in her eye and a knowing smile on her face and say, "Look out for those guys who didn't study in high school."

A Family Tradition?

My mother was a teacher. She was born in the early 1900's, lived on a farm, and attended country school. In those days in rural Minnesota, a sixth grade or eighth grade education was the norm. Since she wanted to become a teacher, she attended high school in Redwood Falls, about eight miles from her family's farm. This was before the days of school buses or of high school kids having cars at their ready disposal and it was too far for her parents to drive her to school in the morning and to pick her up at night. Therefore, she moved in with an aunt in town for the entire school year. When she graduated she was the class valedictorian.

My mother attended Teacher's College for two

years and received her certification to teach. She taught in Wisconsin and Minnesota for several years. I have a copy of a teacher's contract that my mother signed in 1928. The job paid $100 per month for the 9-month school year and the contract contained this stipulation, *"Said teacher agrees not to attend dances nor remain out after 12 midnight on school nights."*

My mother retired from teaching to become a full-time farm wife when she married my father.

Although my mother valued education and considered the teaching profession to be a lofty career, she never talked much about her years as a teacher and never tried to persuade my brother, two sisters, or me to follow in her footsteps. So, that rules out the family tradition as my reason for becoming a teacher.

To Contribute To Society?

I know that a lot of people become teachers for this very reason – to make a positive contribution to society and to help young people learn, grow, and develop. It is truly a worthwhile and admirable reason for becoming a teacher.

When I was about to graduate from high school, just barely seventeen years old, I was not smart enough, philosophical enough, idealistic enough, or mature enough to comprehend the concept of choosing a career because of the good that I could do for others. To be honest, I was interested in choosing a career that could do some good for *me*. So, no, wanting to make a contribution to society was not my reason for becoming a teacher.

My Real Reason For Becoming A Teacher

My reason for becoming a teacher was really quite simple, but I had to think back to my youth and to my days on the farm to figure it out.

Simply stated, my reason for becoming a teacher was *the farm*. I grew up in the era of the small family farm where the entire family worked 10- to 12-hour days Monday through Saturday and worked 4 or 5 hours on Sunday. There were cattle, hogs, and chickens to tend to every morning and night, 7 days a week, 365 days a year. There were crops to plant, cultivate, and harvest and hay to bale and put in the barn during a seven-month season from April to November. There was a huge garden that needed daily attention all summer long. There were weeds to chop in the fields and barns to be cleaned by hand with a fork or shovel. It was brutally hot in the summer and bitterly cold in the winter and we didn't have the air-conditioned tractor cabs in the summer or insulated clothing in the winter that they do now. It was a harsh existence.

I didn't know much about careers or professions that existed out there in the world, but the one career that I had observed first-hand for nearly my entire life was that of teaching. Compared to our life on the farm, the teachers seemed to have it made. As near as I could tell, they showed up for work at 8 a.m. and were done for the day at 3:30 p.m. Out on the farm, we still had half a day's work ahead of us. And, they didn't work Saturdays or Sundays. And, best of all, they had about a month off during the school year for

Christmas vacation, Thanksgiving vacation, Easter vacation, and several other vacations and had three months off in the summer.

So there it is – I chose teaching not because I wanted to be a teacher, but because I wanted the teacher's schedule and lifestyle. Or, should I say, what I perceived to be the teacher's schedule and lifestyle. Boy, was I in for a big surprise.

Choosing a College Major

My high school social studies teacher was a guy named Corliss, who was tremendously excited and enthused about the government and history courses that he taught. So, when I decided that I wanted to be a teacher, I decided that I would be a social science teacher like Corliss. I had not considered the fact that I didn't actually like history and government and that I didn't do particularly well in these classes.

For some reason, that I am not fully aware of, I took a bookkeeping course as an elective my senior year. I was a fair bookkeeping student, earning "B's" throughout the year.

About three weeks before the end of the school year, the teacher gave us a standardized national bookkeeping exam to see how we compared to bookkeeping students around the country. The bookkeeping exam was easy – simple, in fact. Actually, I knew the answer to every single question on the exam. That presented me with a problem. I reasoned that if I, a "B" student, got all of the questions correct, I would be suspected of cheating on the exam, since I had never come close to getting all of the questions correct on any of the exams throughout the year. So, to protect myself from suspicion, I purposefully missed a couple of questions so the test would look more normal for a test taken by me.

When the test results came back about a week before graduation, the results floored the bookkeeping teacher. One of his students had scored in the ninety-ninth percentile – me. Instead of accusing me of cheating on the exam, he took me aside, congratulated me, looked me straight in the eye and said, "If you're going to become a teacher, you should become a business teacher." And, simply, that is why and how I became a business major rather than a social science major.

A College Stoodent

There is a saying that appears on T-shirts on college campuses and in cartoons in college newspapers that says something like, "Fore months ago I couldn't even spell stoodent, and now I are one." That pretty well described me when I entered college at what is now called Minnesota State University.

Looking back at it, most of my college career is a blur. Not because I was into booze or drugs – I wasn't – but because all of my courses, instructors, assignments, tests, and papers just seem to meld together into one gigantic haze. Okay, I did drink a few beers.

Let me summarize my college career by saying that my old high school Principal would have been very surprised. Actually, his revelation in our pre-graduation conference that I had the ability to do well academically if I put my mind to it and studied, changed my life – no one had ever told me that before and I had not suspected it on my own. When I got to college, I studied, hard. I completed my bachelor's degree with a major in Business Education and minors in Business Administration and Physical Education on time in four years.

Although there's nothing particularly noteworthy to mention about most of my college courses, there are a few instances from my college career that stick out in my mind that I would like to share with you.

Registering For Classes

I was green when I left the farm and went off to college. Scared to death. Didn't know what to expect. The fact that *Freshman Orientation* lasted for three days and that we had to wear beanies on our heads for the first three weeks of classes didn't help matters any. I don't recall if our beanies had propellers on them, but I don't think so.

I had received valuable advice about what classes to take from my older brother, Don, who had graduated from the same college several years before. All that good advice went out the window, however, when they herded us freshmen into the basketball gymnasium where hundreds of faculty were seated behind tables waiting to help us register for our first term's classes.

Instead of matching us up with a faculty member from the discipline that we planned to major in, they simply routed us to the next available professor, regardless of their discipline or ours. The guy I ended up with had on a tweed sport coat with leather patches on the elbows, had unruly curly hair, and wore glasses with lenses as thick as Coke bottle bottoms. I immediately nicknamed him McGoo, but only in my mind, of course.

It appeared that McGoo's one goal and only goal in helping me register for classes was to get me the hell out of there so he could get himself the hell out of there.

McGoo grabbed the class schedule, tilted his head back so he could see out of the Coke bottles and started filling in my class schedule. "Let's see," he said, "here's Sociology,

English, History, Intro to Business, and Art Appreciation.

Before I could raise an objection, McGoo signed my registration form, handed it to me, directed me towards the exit, and waved for the next victim to take my place. He wanted to get the hell out of there and I was just one stepping stone closer to his making an exit.

My Personal Faculty Advisor

During the first academic term, each of us freshmen was assigned a faculty advisor, who was a professor who taught in our chosen field of study. My advisor was Dr. Clem Bigelow, who was a business education professor.

The college handbook said that we were to contact our faculty advisor to select courses to take for each term and that our faculty advisor had to sign our registration form in order for us to register for classes. The handbook further stated that our faculty advisor would guide us so that we took the proper courses in the proper order and that the faculty advisor would maintain our official file and keep it up to date.

About three weeks before the start of winter quarter, I stopped in to see Dr. Bigelow to have him help me select the proper courses, but he was not in his office. I made careful note of his posted office hours and stopped back about twenty times over the next two weeks before I finally caught up with him.

Even though the door to his office was wide open, I tapped lightly on the door jam before entering. Dr. Bigelow looked up from his desk and stared at me through wire-rimmed glasses with lenses that resembled the Coke bottle bottoms worn by Professor McGoo.

"So?" he asked.

"I'm one of your advisees," I replied cautiously.

"So?" he asked.

"I want to register for winter quarter classes," I said.

"So?" he asked.

"I'm supposed to have you help me pick the right courses," I replied.

Dr. Bigelow yanked open a desk drawer and withdrew three items. "This is a list of courses you need to graduate with a business education major," he said, handing me a piece of paper with the heading, *Business Education Major*. "This is the winter quarter course offering booklet," he said, handing me the second item, "and this is a registration form. Fill it out and bring it back to me when you're done."

I held the three items in my hand and hesitated for a moment, expecting further directions or assistance.

"So?" he asked.

I finally got the message and slithered out of his office.

That night I analyzed the courses listed in the *Business Education Major* form and pieced together what appeared to be an appropriate schedule of courses for the next term.

It took five tries before I found Dr. Bigelow in his office. I knocked lightly on the door jam before entering. He tilted his head back and looked at me through his Coke bottle glasses.

"So? He asked.

"I'm one of your advisees – I filled out the winter quarter registration form and wondered if you'd take a look at it," I said as I handed it to him.

Dr. Bigelow grabbed a pen and scribbled something at the bottom of the form where the faculty advisor was supposed to sign, without even taking a glance at the courses that I had listed. He pitched the registration form in my direction and was back to work on the project on his desk before the form even hit my hands.

"T-thanks," I mumbled as I backed out of his office. Even though I was a green freshman, I got the message.

That was the last time that I ever approached Dr. Bigelow about registering for classes. From then on, I simply figured out which courses I needed to take, filled in the registration form, scribbled something at the bottom of the form where the faculty advisor was to sign, and turned it in.

A month before I graduated I needed to submit my *Application For Graduation*, which, of course, needed to be signed by my faculty advisor. I toyed with the idea of marching into Dr. Bigelow's office, handing him the application and saying, "So?" Or walking into his office and saying, "Guess who I am?" Or walking into his office and saying "Thanks for all of your help and advisement these past four years."

However, I simply signed Bigelow's signature, turned in the application, and sailed through graduation.

I don't begrudge Dr. Bigelow for being a lousy faculty advisor; in fact, I'm glad that he was. As you may recall, it took about twenty-five visits to his office to get my first registration form signed. Through my college career, I needed to obtain his signature on about fifteen documents, and at that rate it would have required around 375 visits to his office to get all of that done. At an average of twenty minutes per visit to Dr. Bigelow's office, I saved about 125 hours of my precious time by simply signing his name myself. Thanks, Doc.

Just Trying To Have A Little Fun

Yes, I studied hard in college. After my lackluster performance in high school, I had a lot of ground to make up. But, my buddies and I did have some fun along the way, too. I played intramural basketball, was on a bowling team, attended some of the college sporting events, and made it to a couple dozen Rock 'N Roll concerts. And, of course, there were some girls.

Judy, Judy, Judy

When I was a junior in college, and underage, some of my buddies and I would occasionally sneak into one of the college hangouts downtown where this gal Liz played piano and sang songs. Liz was maybe twenty-two years old, beautiful, built, sexy, and engaged to this big, mean-looking sucker. So, we would listen to Liz play piano and sing her songs while we drooled, but that was as close as anybody got to having any interaction, or action, with Liz. Recall that she was engaged to this big mean-looking sucker.

Then, one night, this other beautiful, built, sexy gal showed up and sang a duet with Liz. As it turned out, it was

Liz's sister, Judy. After a little sleuthing, I found out that she, just like me, was a junior in college and was not engaged. In fact, she didn't even have a boyfriend.

Judy was out of my league, there was no doubt of that, but that didn't stop me. I started asking around and finally found an acquaintance of mine who was also an acquaintance of Judy's. After some begging and pleading on my part, this mutual acquaintance finally agreed to put in a good word for me with Judy. After some additional begging and pleading, I finally convinced this mutual acquaintance to ask Judy if she would go on a date with me. The mutual acquaintance must have said some really great, and undoubtedly exaggerated, things about me, because Judy agreed to the date. This thrilled me to no end, but it also shocked me beyond belief. Recall, that even I realized that Judy was out of my league.

Our date was for eight o'clock on Saturday night to go to a movie. The mutual acquaintance phoned me at about two in the afternoon and said that Judy was really excited about the date and was, in fact, already fixing her hair and primping. This thrilled me to no end, but it also shocked me beyond belief, again.

I knocked on the door and was almost knocked over when Judy opened the door and stood there looking like Miss America. I was speechless.

I walked Judy to the car and opened the door for her. So far, so good. I got behind the wheel and looked at Judy – she was smiling at me. I was speechless.

And, much to my embarrassment and disgrace, I,

who eventually became one of the world's great talkers, who normally talks at two hundred words per minute with occasional bursts of three hundred words a minute, remained speechless for the entire evening. No matter how hard I tried, I simply could not think of a single thing to say. What is a guy who's out of his league supposed to say to Miss America, anyway? Nothing, as it turned out. And the longer I went without saying anything, the harder it got to say anything. Oh, I did mumble something like "I enjoyed the date," or something dumb like that when I walked her to the door, but it was too little too late to salvage the evening or to set the stage for a second date.

Fortunately, there were twelve thousand students on campus and I was able to avoid Judy's ever seeing me again. If we had met face to face, I just don't know what I would have said to her. Nothing, probably.

I did see Judy from a distance a couple of times, with a crowd of guys following her like puppy dogs, talking smart, trying to win her favor. Even from a distance I could tell that she was out of their league.

I'm sure that Judy remembers me, so I don't even have to wonder about that. Who could forget a date where the idiot you were out with couldn't utter a single word? I'm sure she has told the story a thousand times, and I don't blame her. I would have told it myself except that I was the idiot. I did write a poem, though, in an effort to cleanse my soul and to wash the memory from my mind.

Ode To Judy
Her name was Judy
And she was a beauty
She fixed her "do" at two
For our date at eight
But it didn't matter anyway
'Cause this tongue-tied idiot couldn't think of a thing to say
And now some other dude
Is dating my Jude

Okay, so Edgar Allan Shakespeare I ain't, but it made me feel a little better, knowing that I had finally faced up to it.

Years after my ill-fated date with Judy, I read an article in a medical magazine that might explain what happened that night on that date. It's called *Selective Mutism*. That is, a condition whereby under certain circumstances, a person who normally can talk like a normal person is rendered mute. In my case, apparently, selective mutism hits when I'm on a date with a beautiful woman of Miss America caliber who is obviously out of my league.

So, Judy, if you're reading this, now you, too, know why I was unable to talk that night - I suffer from a rare, severe, and uncontrollable medical condition, that although usually not fatal, can be extremely humiliating – especially when a guy like me knows that he's out of his league.

A Few More College Daze Stories

Oh, there are a few more stories that I could share

with you about my college days, but they're probably not a whole lot different than most people's stories. Except maybe for that Saturday morning I was on my way to purchase a set of pearl-coated bongos when my parents intercepted me and administered a stern lecture about cutting back on my excessive spending. So much for the bongos. Or perhaps the Teaching Rhythms course that I took where I had the entire class stomping around in a circle dancing to the syllables of my name as I shouted to a rhythmic beat, "Da-vid, Pe-ter-son, Da-vid Pe-ter-son." Or I suppose I could have told you about that *Mountain Brew* beer at $2.19 a case – every bottle a slightly different color. But, as they say, that's an entirely different story.

Job Hunting

The process of applying for my first teaching job started around April of my senior year in college, when it appeared that I was most likely going to graduate that spring. The process was really quite simple. Schools that needed a business teacher notified the college placement office and the placement office posted the openings for everyone to see.

If a job looked interesting, you'd send a letter and résumé to the school that had an opening. If the school was impressed by your letter and résumé, or if they were desperate, they'd call you in for a personal interview. If that went well, they'd offer you the job. If the offer looked good, or if you were desperate, you'd take it.

I fired off letters to every school that had an opening regardless if they were big or small, near or far. This took several evenings per week, since this was before the era of computers or photocopy machines and I had to create every letter and every résumé individually on a typewriter.

A College Graduate – And Back To The Farm

I graduated from college without having a teaching job lined up and went back home to help my dad on the farm for the summer. And, it appeared that maybe I'd be on the farm for more than the summer – like forever. How ironic was that?

Occasionally, the college placement office sent me a new opening that I applied for immediately, but as the end of June approached, the number of new openings dwindled. It appeared that most schools had their teaching positions filled and the only new ones that came open were flukes where a teacher had suddenly resigned because of ill health or because they were unexpectedly offered a job in the business world that they couldn't pass up.

Prospects of obtaining a teaching position were starting to appear bleak and I was grateful that I had majored in business, which might enable me to get a job in the real world. I didn't realize until then, when it appeared that I probably wasn't going to become a teacher, how badly I actually wanted to become one.

Finally, in early July, a friend who had graduated a year ahead of me and who was teaching in a small town just thirty miles from where I went to college, called. The business teacher had suddenly resigned and my friend had put in a good word for me with the Superintendent. She told me to phone him immediately. I did, and the Superintendent invited me for an interview. The interview went well, and I was offered the job. I accepted on the spot. It was a case of two desperate parties needing each other and solving their problems simultaneously in one fell swoop.

Later in July, and again in August, I received phone calls from two schools desperately in need of a business teacher for the upcoming school year. I believe they would have offered me the job over the phone, sight unseen. I realize that I was offered the teaching position that I accepted largely because of the recommendation of a friend. It was heartening to know that I could have obtained a job on my own.

I did not have a car of my own in high school or in college. I used my parents' car when I was at home and I had generous roommates and friends at college who would give me a ride or loan me their car if I really needed one.

My dad had promised me that when I graduated from college he would buy me a brand new car and I could pay him for it little by little whenever I could. He was a man of his word and I got my new car in July – a bright red two door Chevy hardtop. It was worth the wait.

As the summer passed, I counted the days that I had left until I would leave the farm behind me for good and would embark on what I considered to be a more leisurely career as a teacher. In late August, I loaded all of my worldly possessions into my new car and headed off to my new life. I had looked forward to this day ever since I was in high school and now my dream was coming true.

I have never revealed this to anyone, but when I got about three miles down the road, the reality of my leaving home for good hit me hard and I burst into tears and cried like a baby for the next twenty miles. I thought of turning around and going back home, but I could not, for I was no longer a farmer – I was a teacher and I would soon have students who would be eager to have me teach them the vast knowledge and wisdom that I possessed. Or, more accurately, I should say, the vast knowledge and wisdom that they *thought* I possessed.

This Is Teaching? (Faculty In-Service)

My first activity as a brand new high school business teacher was to attend two days of faculty *in-service*, which is often referred to as *workshop* in teacher jargon. In my four years of college training to become a business educator, no one had ever mentioned in-service. I had no idea what to expect.

The first day of in-service was for those of us who were new to the school system. The Principal greeted us warmly, discussed a few rules and regulations with us, issued us grade books and lesson plan books, and described how to use them.

The business manager had us fill out some employment forms and described that we could take our paychecks in nine or twelve monthly installments. I chose twelve, assuming that if I took my pay in nine installments, I'd be broke when June rolled around and I'd be back on the farm for the summer. We had the afternoon to ourselves to prepare for classes, which started in two days.

The second day of in-service was for the entire faculty and began with a continental breakfast. The atmosphere resembled a party as returning teachers caught up with one another after having been off for the summer.

The main topic for this day was the *Title III grant*, which was also something that they had failed to mention during my four years of college education. Whatever the Title III grant was, it must have been important since the Superintendent himself led the discussion of the topic. After a half-hour jumbled explanation, the Superintendent turned us loose to go to our classrooms to complete the Title III grant applications with instructions to return them to the Principal's office by the end of the day.

The social science teacher, a guy named Gundy, must have noticed my bewilderment and he took it upon himself to explain the Title III program to me in plain English and to guide me in completing my portion of the application. According to Gundy, Title III was a three-year grant program through which the federal government gave money to the schools to buy equipment. The program had already been in effect for one year and we were to complete applications for the second year of the program. Each discipline had been given a budget showing how many dollars worth of equipment we could purchase under the Title III program. My budget was four thousand dollars, which was a lot of money in those days.

I'll admit that I was fresh off the farm and hadn't been around much and was naïve. What Gundy told me next stunned me. He said that I had to spend the full four thousand dollars that I had been allotted, even if I bought stuff that I really didn't need, because if we didn't spend all of this year's money, next year's money would be reduced to the amount that we spent this year.

To prove his point, Gundy took me to a storeroom where teacher's desks were piled three high, four wide, and six deep. Since the lifetime of a teacher's desk is about fifty years, there were enough desks there to meet the school's needs for the next three hundred years.

Since my predecessor had spent all of the first year's Title III money that he had been allotted, the Business Department was fully equipped with modern, up-to-date equipment. I had a tough time spending my entire allotted budget, but I did it. I dreaded the following year when I would be forced to spend more money on things that my department didn't need.

Thus was my introduction to the world of government programs and to the wild spending that often results from them.

ooooo

I taught in that high school four years and the in-service each year was similar to that first year. The Principal covered a few rules and regulations, we completed whatever paperwork was necessary, and we had the rest of the time to ourselves to prepare for our classes. It was practical and painless.

Whoda Thunk It – A College Professor

The high school that I taught at was thirty miles from Minnesota State University, and I began working on my master's degree in business during my second year of teaching. Through a combination of night classes and summer sessions, and writing my Master's thesis at the same time, I completed my Master's degree in two years, while continuing to teach full time. I taught high school one more year before leaving to teach business courses at Lakes Community College. I was twenty-five years old.

Faculty In-Service, College Style

My first activity as a new teacher at Lakes Community College was to attend faculty in-service. The first day was similar to my first day of in-service at the high school level – a friendly greeting, a few rules and regulations, a little paperwork to take care of, and some time to prepare for classes. The remainder of in-service caught me by surprise – there was an agenda listing four solid days of meetings. I was about to be introduced to a whole new meaning of the term, *in-service*.

Speakers with great credentials and résumé's that were sometimes thirty pages long were brought in from around the country to expose us to their wisdom. Their topics included things like "The Role of Community Colleges in Society," " The Philosophy of Higher Education," and "The Educational Matrix at Work." For the most part, the presentations were long on philosophy and short on practicality. And, they were just plain long. And boring. It was widely understood that if you could survive the week of in-service, the rest of the year was a snap.

∞∞∞

About my fourth year at Lakes Community College, I created a ritual that very pleasantly occupied at least a half day of in-service and that I followed religiously until the time that I retired thirty years later.

There was always a coffee pot with white Styrofoam cups available each morning of in-service. On the first day, I would get my cup of coffee, take a seat as far back in the auditorium as I could, and leisurely drink my coffee down to the very last drop. Then, as the first speaker started blazing away, I would grab my pen and start decorating my Styrofoam cup. Actually, decorating isn't the proper term. I turned the cup into a journal as I recorded personal activities and events that had occurred the past summer, activities that I was currently working on, plans that I had for the future, and times, dates, and places of significance to me at that time. I recorded my thoughts on the outside of the cup, the inside, the bottom – everywhere.

When I retired, I filled more than a dumpster with

discarded materials that I carted out of my office and an adjoining classroom that was lined with cabinets. I loaded a few boxes of good stuff into my car and took it home. Among the good stuff were thirty Styrofoam cup-journals. I can pick any one of them at random, study it for a few minutes, and be reminded of exactly what was going on in my life at that time. They are among my most valued treasures and best memories of my years as a teacher.

ooooo

I do have a few fond memories of several in-service moments. For instance, there was the time that a speaker placed a transparency on the overhead that projected the image of intersecting vertical and horizontal lines forming squares on a huge screen in the front of the auditorium. "How many of you can see the horizontal lines?" he asked. Everyone in the place raised their hands. "How many of you can see the vertical lines?" he asked. Everyone in the place raised their hands. "How many of you can see the diagonal lines?" he asked.

I squinted at the screen but try as I might, I couldn't see the damn lines. Hands were going up all over the place and I was thinking of joining the crowd just so I didn't look foolish because I couldn't see the lines when the speaker said, "There aren't any."

I don't recall what the speaker's point was, or even if there was one, but it did seem to prove that you can make people believe just about anything if you present it properly.

◌◌◌◌

Another speaker projected on the screen a picture of a drinking glass that contained water to the halfway point. "Would you say this glass is half full – or half empty?" he asked the group. Apparently he was trying to demonstrate that optimists would say its half full and pessimists would say it's half empty. He never got the chance to explain what he was up to because the Philosophy teacher stopped him dead in his tracks when he shouted, "You simply got too big of a glass."

◌◌◌◌

About three-fourths of the in-service presenters had backgrounds in psychology or philosophy. Through the years of attending in-service sessions presented by them, I came to believe that most of them were weird and the rest were just plain sick. This was evidenced by the fact that their favorite in-service technique was to get us into small groups of six or eight people and then to give us a topic to discuss with each other where we were to spill our guts. Some topics that I recall were, "Complete this sentence – The favorite part of my body is…," "My most horrible experience as a child was…," "The thing I hate most about teaching is…," and "My worst personal trait is…" Weird? Sick? You decide.

In all the years that I taught, I figure that I attended around 136 days of teacher in-service and sat through nearly 1,000 hours of presentations. Not once do I recall any of the presentations dealing with teaching.

Students

Students – those wonderful, brilliant, zany, maddening, idiotic, inspired, lazy, ambitious, lethargic, nutcases who fill the chairs in classrooms and create jobs for teachers. They are all of these things, and more.

Regardless of the reason that a person chose a teaching career, the reason that they stayed in the profession most likely is the *students*. They inspire and motivate teachers, they perplex and bewilder teachers, and they dumbfound and amaze them. Their failures cause teachers great anguish, and their successes are a teacher's greatest rewards. And, students provide teachers with fodder for some wonderful and wacky stories. This section of the book is about those stories.

Harold

Harold was a borderline high school student, teetering between belonging in the regular classes and being better off in the special education program. Mostly, he took the regular classes with the rest of the students. I suspect a lot of teachers simply passed him so they wouldn't have to deal with him again the next year.

Harold had several social disorders, but one in particular was unusual. Once in a while, if someone said a word, it was kind of like a secret word that set Harold off. For instance, one day a teacher walked into class and said hoarsely, "I'm sorry if my voice doesn't carry well today because I have a cold."

That set Harold off. "Cold!" he shouted. "I'll tell you about being cold. One winter night I got locked out of the house wearing nothing but a pair of shorts and tee shirt and it was twenty below and I was out there for over a half hour – that's cold."

Another time a teacher said, "Working at a second job in addition to a regular job is called *moonlighting*."

"Moonlight!" Harold shouted. "When there's a full moon it can drive some people crazy, especially if they're nuts to begin with."

Once in a while Harold would fixate on a word and use it three or four times in every sentence, regardless of the topic. There was the time, for instance, when the word, *particular*, got stuck in his mind. He would say things like, "On this one particular day I had this particular errand to run so I went to this particular store to get the particular stuff that I needed for some particular reason."

Usually, after a few days, Harold would wear the word out and stop using it, or another word would get stuck in his mind and replace it.

Even though Harold's antics could be pretty wearing, most of the time you could ignore him and write him off as being harmless. That is, until one day Harold was overheard using an obscene word over and over in his conversation. It was "this c***sucker," "that c***sucker," "them c***suckers," "you c***sucker," "they're c***suckers," "c***sucker, c***sucker, c***sucker," all day long.

Sometimes, as in this case, Harold really didn't know what he was saying and didn't know that he was using a bad word. Perhaps, like a child, he heard someone use the word and thought it sounded cool, so he used it over and over. Or maybe it got stuck in his mind and wouldn't go away.

A couple of teachers reported Harold's antics to the Principal. Since Harold was embarrassing himself, even though he didn't realize it, and was embarrassing everyone around him by his constant use of the "C word," the Principal decided to have a little talk with Harold and to get him to stop using that word.

Although Harold was a little slow, a little unusual, and had some odd traits, he was very respectful of authority. The Principal called Harold into his office and told him to sit down. Harold obeyed. The Principal closed the door and took his seat behind his desk. Harold hung his head like a naughty boy who knew he had been caught doing something wrong. Since Harold had been called into the Principal's office, even he could assume that he had done something wrong, but, Harold being Harold, had no clue as to what it was.

The Principal began slowly, intent on informing Harold about his bad choice of words and on getting him to stop using the word. The Principal was also cautious not to offend or upset Harold, since he undoubtedly had no idea he was using a bad word and sometimes when he became upset Harold would fall to pieces.

"Harold," the Principal said, "I've been told that you have been using a word the last couple of days that is a bad word and a word that you shouldn't say."

Harold hung his head lower. His eyes looked straight down at the floor. He was embarrassed and afraid that the Principal was about to punish him.

"You probably don't know that it is a bad word, Harold," the Principal continued, "and I'm not mad at you and am not going to punish you. But the bad word that you've been using is…" The Principal paused for a moment, partly because he felt awkward saying the word and partly for effect. "…c***sucker," he finally said quietly.

Harold hung his head even lower. Obviously he didn't know that it was a bad word.

"Did you know that is a bad word, Harold, that c***sucker is a bad word?" the Principal asked.

Harold shook his head, slowly, sadly.

"Do you understand now that is a bad word?" he asked Harold.

He nodded his head, slowly, sadly.

"Do you understand that you shouldn't use that word anymore?" the Principal asked

Harold nodded his head.

"You can go now, Harold," the Principal said, "but just don't use that word any more."

Harold slowly raised his head and looked at the Principal with eyes filled with gratitude. It was hard to tell if that gratitude was for telling him about the bad word that he had been using or if it was for not punishing him, but Harold was grateful.

The Principal rose and Harold likewise rose from his chair and slowly and timidly opened the door, walked out, and closed the door behind him.

About fifteen seconds later, Harold opened the door to the Principal's office, stuck his head in, looked the Principal squarely in the eye and said, "c***sucker."

Investigative Reporters

The Journalism program at Lakes Community College was taught by a man who had been a reporter for several newspapers and had broken a big story or two in his day. The students applied their newly learned journalism skills by writing stories for the weekly college newspaper.

Young minds are often as pliable as Silly Putty, especially when they want to believe what they are being told. The Journalism instructor convinced them that they were not merely reporters, but that they were *investigative reporters* who had the responsibility to expose wrongdoing, uncover big secrets, and ferret out behind-the-scenes back room dealing. They lurked around campus, note pad in hand, searching for that big story that they could break in the college newspaper.

Often, one of the investigative reporters would approach a faculty member and strike up a friendly, non-threatening conversation like, "Nice day, isn't it!" "That was a great game last night, wasn't it!" "You really enjoy teaching, don't you!" and "I'll bet that coat of yours is really warm, isn't it!"

Then, after posing a series of simple comments to which you would agree, "Yes," "Yes," "Yes," "Yes," they would slip in a hard-edged question like, "The College President is a real son-of-a-bitch, isn't he!" They'd whip out their note pad and pen in the hope that they had lulled you into the habit of saying "Yes," and that you'd say "Yes" one more time and give them a quotable quote. If you weren't on your toes, the headline in the next college newspaper might scream something like, PROFESSOR PETERSON CALLS COLLEGE PRESIDENT A SON-OF-A-BITCH!

Nothing or no one was off limits to the investigative reporters. They finally came up with what they thought would be their big story and they followed the college President around day and night with a camera, trying to catch him using the college car for personal use, which would be an illegal use of public property and could even result in jail time. If they could break that story, it might get picked up by every newspaper in the state and maybe even by the Associated Press, and they'd be on their way to the big time.

Apparently, the President was onto them, however, and had his guard up. After hounding the President for a couple of weeks and getting nothing on him, they gave up investigative reporting and went back to writing nice little stories for the college newspaper complaining about the quality of food in the cafeteria, arguing that teachers gave too many tests, and campaigning for the sale of beer in the college bookstore.

It was nice to again be able to meet one of the journalism students in the hallway and to have them say, "Hello," without wondering what in the hell they were up to.

The Mass Cut

When I was a college student, occasionally somebody would organize a *mass cut*, where all of us students would stay away from a certain class on a given day. There was strength in numbers and nobody got into any trouble over it. Usually, when that class met the next time, the professor would say something like, "Okay, you've had your fun," which meant, "It was okay to do it once, but don't do it again."

When I taught at Lakes Community College, the students would likewise occasionally organize a mass cut. I'd show up for class on time, and no one was there. I would quietly smile to myself, offer them silent congratulations, and go enjoy a cup of coffee. One class session more or less didn't matter much. I probably enjoyed the time off from the mass cut as much as the students. Then when that class met the next time, I'd say something like, "Okay, you've had your fun," which meant, "It was okay to do it once, but don't do it again."

I taught a class in accounting that met on Monday, Wednesday, and Friday at 2 p.m. There were about thirty students in the class and it was, for all practical purposes, a typical group of students.

One day, I showed up for class and there was no one there. "Mass cut," I said to myself silently with a little smile on my lips as I started to pack up my stuff and head for an unexpected cup of coffee.

About the time that I was about to exit the room, one of my students, Andrew, walked in, looked around as though he was amazed that no one was there, and took his seat. It appeared that they had forgotten to clue Andrew in on the plans for a mass cut. Before I could tell Andrew to hit the bricks, the rest of the students started to file in, slowly and clearly downhearted. Trying to pull off a mass cut that fails can put you in a bad mood.

About a week later, I walked into my classroom and it was empty. "All right," I said to myself. They had gotten their act together and had pulled off the mass cut. I started to pack up my stuff so I could go grab that cup of coffee when Andrew walked into the room, looked around as though he was amazed that no one was there, and took his seat.

Now, leaving Andrew out of the plan for a mass cut once would be an oversight, but leaving him out of the loop twice seemed to be a little more than a coincidence. Was somebody setting him up?

A few minutes later, the rest of the students started to file in, slowly and more than a little downhearted. A couple of them gave Andrew looks that would kill. Why blame him because somebody forgot to clue him in?

About a week later, I walked into my classroom and it was empty, again. "Finally," I thought to myself, "they did it." I started to pack up my stuff so I could have that well-deserved and overdue cup of coffee when Andrew walked into the room, looked around as though he was amazed that no one else was there, and took his seat.

All of a sudden, I understood. Andrew had not been left out of the loop by coincidence or by someone who was trying to set him up as the bad guy. Andrew was fully aware each time that the class had organized a mass cut and he had snuck back into the room to try to curry my favor as the "good" student while he figured that I would consider the rest of the students to be "bad."

A few minutes later, the rest of the students started to file in, very slowly. This time they weren't downhearted, they were thoroughly pissed off. Everyone who walked in shot daggers at Andrew and one young lady walked up to him, stuck her finger in his face and yelled, "You sneaky, sick son-of-a-bitch." That pretty well summed it up.

The class continued on for another couple of weeks without further attempts at a mass cut. The chemistry that had originally existed in the class had totally evaporated. The tension was so thick that you could see it and taste it. Andrew was clearly ostracized from the group and when he sat down, others would inch their chairs away from him.

One day about three weeks before the end of the semester, I showed up for class and no one was there. I waited the unofficial waiting period of five minutes before declaring it a bona fide, official mass cut. I hurriedly packed up my stuff and raced out of the room before Andrew cracked and showed up, ruining everything. I hurried down the hallway and into the faculty lounge, grabbed a cup of coffee, and sunk into an old chair. They had done it; they had finally done it. They had pulled off a genuine, certifiable mass cut. And I finally got that cup of coffee that I had been thinking about ever since they had tried to pull off the first mass cut some six weeks before.

I don't know if they hog-tied Andrew, threatened him, beat him, or simply took him aside and explained the facts of life to him. Whatever it was, it worked.

I walked into the room the next time class met, smiled and said, "Well, you had your fun," which meant, "It was okay to do it once, but don't do it again." I don't think that my little warning was necessary, I doubt that any of them wanted to go through all of that again, anyway.

If you are a college student and are reading this, be assured that pulling a mass cut is your undeniable God-given right, and also be assured that your teacher will enjoy the mass cut just as much as you, if not more. But, once you've had your fun…

Course Syllabus

We were required to make a course syllabus for each course that we taught and to distribute copies to students on the first day of class. The syllabus listed things like the Course Description, Course Rationale, Course Objectives, Course Content, Attendance Policy, and Grading Scale.

During my first few years, I labored over each syllabus, trying to create a masterpiece that would present valuable information for the students and that would provide a guide that they would refer to time after time throughout the semester. One small event showed me that all of my labors were in vain.

I taught a beginning keyboarding class, designed to teach students how to type using the *Touch Method*, which means typing using the correct fingers on the correct keys without looking at your fingers. In the Course Rationale section of the syllabus, where I justified why this course was offered and why students should take it, I stated, "In today's business world where a computer is used to create correspondence and to do other word processing, it is important to have a good command of the kdybroad." In case you missed it, the last word is spelled KDYBROAD. So much for the *masterpiece*.

Not a single student caught the snafu. And you just know that if they had seen it they would have pointed it out to everyone in the class, and on campus, and probably would have delighted in drilling me as well. That was the moment that I decided from then on I would strive to create a *good* syllabus for each class, but not a *great* one. *Good* would be good enough when nobody reads it anyway.

Class Attendance Policy

At Lakes Community College, each teacher was required to devise an attendance policy for each course and to make it known to the students as part of the course syllabus. In my courses, attendance counted ten percent of the final grade. I allowed students one *unexcused absence* for each credit hour of the course. Therefore, in a three-credit hour course, they could miss three times for any reason or no reason at all without penalty and they would receive an "A" for attendance. The rest of my grading scale for unexcused absences was 4 cuts

= "B," 5 or 6 cuts = "C," 7 cuts = "D," and over seven cuts, Flunko.

I basically allowed students unlimited *excused absences* for missing class because of a serious illness, family emergency, or other unavoidable absences that were not of their own making. I was a pushover and all they had to do was tell me that they missed class because they were violently ill, had an unexpected operation, had a near death experience, or some other tall tale. I chose to believe whatever they told me rather than to hold their feet to the fire to make them confess or trying to double-check their story.

Some students had an unbelievable number of illnesses and calamities and racked up a huge number of excused absences, along with a batch of unexcused absences, missing maybe a third or a half of the class. They thought that they were pulling something on me, but for most students, it is virtually impossible to pass a college course by missing that much of the course and in the end, the joke was on them.

Sammy the Sometime Student

Sammy was one of those students who had really good intentions, but who had trouble with the follow-through. The first course of mine that he signed up for was Sales Principles. He made it to class the first two times that it met and was then absent for about three weeks. Sammy finally showed up and explained that he had been waylaid by a multitude of problems but that he now had everything under control and would be able to attend class regularly from now on. I told him that I'd work with him and not penalize him for his past absences if he attended regularly from then on. He assured me that would be no problem, or as he said it, "No problem at all."

Sammy made it to class the next day and then he didn't show up for another four weeks. When I was about ready to count Sammy out, he showed up and explained that although he had thought that he had things under control, he hadn't, but that he now did. He begged for another chance and I agreed to work with him.

Sammy actually made it to two of the next three class meetings. Then I didn't see him again until two weeks before the end of the semester when he came in to have me sign his course drop slip.

Much to my surprise, Sammy signed up for another of my classes the following semester. It was an exact duplicate of the previous class where Sammy showed up a time or two, disappeared for weeks, showed up again, disappeared for weeks, showed up again, and finally dropped the class.

When classes began the following fall semester, to my amazement, there was Sammy, again. Sammy apparently saw the skeptical look in my eye when he walked into the classroom, so he approached me after class and told me that he was a reborn student and that I could expect to see him in class every day, "No problem." Well, that lasted about two weeks and Sammy again ended up dropping the class.

To my continued amazement, when I checked my class list the day before spring semester started, Sammy was again signed up for one of my classes. I liked Sammy; he was a good guy, but it was obvious that my current attendance policy was doing nothing to encourage, or threaten, Sammy enough to entice him to attend class regularly. But, I had an idea.

Sammy was there for the first day of class, which was his custom. As usual, I handed out the course syllabus, explained everything on it to the students, gave them a reading assignment for the next class, and turned them loose.

I grabbed Sammy and led him into my office and told him to have a chair. I said, "Sammy, you have signed up for three of my courses before this one and your total attendance in all three courses could be counted on your fingers of both hands."

Sammy grinned and nodded his head in agreement.

"Well, Sammy," I said, "I have a special attendance policy for you," as I handed him a sheet of paper. Sammy's special attendance policy read as follows.

AGREEMENT

This agreement is entered into between David Peterson, a Professor at Lakes Community College and hereinafter referred to as THE PROFESSOR, and Sammy, a student at Lakes Community College, hereinafter referred to as THE STUDENT.

WHEREAS THE PROFESSOR is instructor of the Advertising Principles course, hereinafter identified as THE COURSE, and THE STUDENT is enrolled in THE COURSE.

WHEREAS in the past the standard attendance policy for courses taught by THE PROFESSOR and taken by THE STUDENT have been highly ineffective in encouraging THE STUDENT to attend classes.

THEREFORE, the following special attendance policy shall be in effect between THE PROFESSOR and THE STUDENT for THE COURSE:

THE PROFESSOR shall pay to THE STUDENT the sum of TWO DOLLARS ($2.00) for each time that THE STUDENT attends a class session of THE COURSE.

THE STUDENT shall pay to THE PROFESSOR the sum of ONE DOLLAR ($1.00) for each time that THE STUDENT misses a class session of THE COURSE.

Final settlement of the amount owed between THE PROFESSOR and THE STUDENT shall be made on the day of the final exam for THE COURSE.

This document contains the full and complete agreement between THE PROFESSOR and THE STUDENT.

Signed this tenth day of January, 2005.

_____   _____

David Peterson (THE PROFESSOR)   Sammy (THE STUDENT)

Sammy read the agreement intently and then looked at me and smiled. "Are you serious?" he asked.

"As serious as getting run over by a cement truck," I replied.

"How many times does the course meet during the semester?" he asked. It is the first time that I saw Sammy express an interest in anything connected to one of my courses in the year and a half that I had known him.

"It meets three times a week for fifteen weeks – forty-five times," I said.

"You'd pay me two dollars a class for forty-five classes? That's, uh..."

"Ninety dollars," I said.

"You'd pay me ninety dollars if I attend all of the classes?"

"That's right – but remember you'll have to pay me a dollar for each time you miss class – you could actually end up owing *me* money if you miss class as much as you have in the past," I explained.

"No way," Sammy said with a smile as he eagerly signed the agreement. He was already spending the money.

Sammy attended the first four times that class met. It looked like the special attendance policy was working. As Sammy walked out of the classroom that day, he held up four fingers and mouthed the words, "Eight bucks," as a huge smile played upon his lips.

I didn't see Sammy again for four weeks, after he had missed twelve classes in a row and now owed me a net of four dollars. Sammy explained why he had missed class – some pretty wonderful reasons, all – and vowed to never miss again the rest of the semester. He attended class two times in a row and then never showed up again – he didn't even bother to stop in to have me sign a class drop slip. I suppose that he figured I'd put the bite on him for the money that he owed me.

The final tally was he attended class six times and earned $12 and missed class thirty-nine times and owed me $39 – a net due of $27. Sammy didn't know it, but I didn't intend to collect; the agreement was just a tactic to try to get him to attend class. I would have paid, though, if I had owed him money.

The special attendance policy for THE COURSE may have failed miserably, but in the long run it worked fabulously – Sammy never took another course from me again, ever.

Classroom Pranksters

In most of the classes that I taught, students would file into the room, take their seats, stay there until the class was over, and file back out. In the meantime, some of them listened, some of them participated in class discussions, some of them took notes, some of them doodled, some of them slept, some of them whispered to their neighbor, some of them passed notes back and forth, some of them paved the road to success, and some of them were on a bumpy trail to failure.

Occasionally a student, or the entire class, would pull a prank, which was usually designed to tease, taunt, or compliment the teacher. Of all the pranks that students pulled on me or that I heard they pulled on other teachers, I never heard of one that was mean-spirited, demeaning, or humiliating. The students were simply trying to have a little good-natured fun.

I recall one day that I walked into my classroom and was greeted by about thirty students sitting very quietly wearing grocery bags on their heads with holes cut out for their eyes and nose. A crisp new sack lay on the desk in the front of the room. Evidently, it was for me. I played along with them and put the bag on my head. I tried to read the class role, but I couldn't see out of the holes in the bag so I had to remove the bag. The students wore the bags on their heads for around a half hour before removing them. I still have my grocery bag in my boxes of mementos.

Some years ago on a nice warm spring day, someone pounded loudly on the window in the back of my classroom. All of the students, of course, turned around to see what was going on and were greeted by someone's bare butt pressed up against the window. The image lasted for only a second or two and I pretended not to see it as I continued on with my lecture without missing a beat, until a girl in the class exclaimed, "Mr. Peterson, did you see *that*!" The class went nuts.

The mooning incident caused a little excitement in class, it was recognized as a college prank, and it was soon forgotten. No real harm done. If someone tried that today, it would trigger a full-scale investigation and if the perpetrator were caught, they'd probably do hard time in the slammer for indecent exposure, sexual harassment, and several other things. It was a simpler time back then.

The high school students told me about this prank, and

I don't think that the teacher involved ever figured it out. The classroom had large windows with curtains on them. In the morning when the sun was beating down, the teacher always closed the curtains. Bob was a slender student and he would frequently arrive in the classroom before the teacher and would climb up in the window and hide behind the closed curtain.

At the start of class, precisely 10 a.m., the teacher would shut the door. The teacher was a stickler for attendance; every student had an assigned seat and the teacher took attendance by simply noting the empty chairs. Often, Bob's chair would be empty and the teacher would mark him down as being absent. Then, when the teacher turned around to write on the board, Bob would emerge from his hiding place and when the teacher turned around, whoa, there was Bob.

In another high school class, the entire class would slide their chairs back about an inch every time the teacher turned around to write on the board. By the end of a class session, the students had often moved back two feet or more. Towards the end of class, the teacher would sometimes look at the students like, "Something's wrong with this picture, but I'm not exactly sure what it is."

ooooo

My friend, Cliff, was considered to be the top high school Spanish teacher in the state and he was beloved by his students, and by the parents, faculty, administration, and community. When he announced his retirement, it sent shock waves through the community. It was particularly unsettling for the Spanish students that *Senor*, as he was known, was leaving.

The advanced Spanish class, made up of all seniors, wanted to do something special to honor him. They proposed an idea to the senior class and they all agreed. They asked *Senor* if he would lead the senior class into the auditorium for their graduation ceremony.

After careful thought, *Senor* declined saying that there were others retiring that same year and he didn't think it would be right to single himself out for special recognition. This did not sit well with the advanced Spanish class for they loved *Senor* and wanted to honor him.

The next day when *Senor* showed up to teach his class, the advanced Spanish students had all turned their chairs to face the back of the room. Unfazed, *Senor* charged ahead with the day's lesson, lecturing, writing on the board, and involving students without asking the students what they were doing, without asking them to turn around, and without reprimanding them. No wonder they loved him so.

Turning The Tables

Occasionally, I got the chance to turn the tables on a student and to be the classroom prankster. I often joked that entertainment hypnotists who called a half dozen people to the stage to be hypnotized had nothing on me – I was capable of putting a whole room full of students out at a time. That was only a joke, ahem, but there were times that a student would fall asleep so soundly in class that you could have detonated a bomb under their chair and they wouldn't have heard it. On occasions like that, if it was near the end of the class hour, I would hold my finger to my lips indicating that the students should be silent, would point to the sleeping beauty, and would motion for the students to quietly exit the room. The students always enjoyed playing along and often we would all get out of the room without the sleepyhead waking up. The final touch was to turn off the lights and to quietly close the door.

Most of the classes that I taught were in the room adjoining my office. There was a large window in the wall between my office and the back of the classroom, allowing me full view of the classroom from my office. After sneaking out of the room, I could stand in my office and watch the sleeping beauty. Often, students who had been in the class would stop in for a peek and I would invite fellow faculty members into my office to witness the results of my hypnotic powers.

If there wasn't another class in that classroom the following period, it was fun to see how long the sleeper would sleep before coming to. Usually, though, there was another class in that room the following hour and the student would wake up when the instructor walked in and turned on the lights. It was always fun to watch the student's reaction when that happened, as they would suddenly come awake and try to comprehend what was going on. You could just imagine that their fuzzy minds were saying, "Where the hell am I?" "What happened?" "Where are the rest of the students?" "What time is it?"

One of my accomplishments as a teacher that I am most proud of is that I once put out a student so thoroughly that he slept in the classroom for twenty-one minutes after the rest of the class and I exited the room. Now, that's power.

Student Demonstrations

No, I'm not talking about marching-on-the administration, tipping over cars, burning the flag, yelling-and-screaming-out-in-the-street kinds of demonstrations. I'm talking about the type of demonstrations that my Sales Principles students made when they gave an in-class sales presentation and the demonstrations staged by the Speech students when they gave a demonstration speech. The Speech teacher and I were friends and we would often compare notes about the demonstrations that our students gave in class.

As part of the Sales Principles class that I taught, students were required to select a product or service and to make an in-class sales presentation to another student who would act as the buyer. The sales presentation was to include a demonstration, where the seller would show the product in action. The sales presentation counted as one-fifth of the seller's grade in the course. The grade received by the student was largely dependent upon two things – the amount of resistance offered by the buyer, thus allowing the seller to show their stuff, and the sales demonstration.

There were some sales presentations, literally, where the

seller started out by saying something like, "I'm selling these here shoes and I don't suppose you'd like to buy a pair," to which his student buyer would say, "Ya, I'll take two." End of the sales presentation, and end of the seller's grade.

There were other presentations where the buyer raised numerous realistic questions and objections and made the seller extend him or herself and gave them a chance to show what they could do.

The demonstrations were often the most interesting part of the sales presentations. I recall one student who demonstrated a vacuum cleaner. He described the setting for the sales presentation as being in the buyer's home in the living room. The seller started out by talking about the vacuum cleaner's many features and how each of them translated into a benefit for the buyer. Great start.

After describing the tremendous suction and power that his vacuum cleaner had, the seller set out to demonstrate that which he said was true. Great technique.

He took a bag out of his briefcase and poured its contents, a powder of some sort, onto the buyer's living room rug, which in reality was the carpet in my classroom. Then, he brought out his mighty vacuum cleaner. He ran that vacuum cleaner back and forth over the powder on the carpet and the only thing that his mighty machine seemed to do was to drive the powder deeper into the carpet. He continued, back and forth, back and forth, but still the powder defeated his mighty vacuum. Undeterred, our salesman proceeded with his presentation as though his vacuum had actually worked and his buyer played along with him. I gave the salesman an "A" on his presentation, for his acting ability and quick thinking, if nothing else.

The custodians used their industrial strength vacuum cleaners on the powder, but they, too, were soundly defeated. They even tried a carpet shampooer, which failed miserably. The powder remained on the floor in my classroom for over ten years and served as a reminder of a sales demonstration that had gone terribly wrong. I got a lot of mileage out of that soiled piece of carpet, however, as I used it to point out to following Sales Principles students what can happen if you don't practice your demonstration in advance to be sure it will actually work. Eventually, the powder disappeared – about ten years later, when they replaced the carpet in the room.

Another student, weighing about 250 pounds, sold a set of luggage and demonstrated its strength and durability by laying it on the floor and by jumping up and down on it. Point well made – he got his "A."

Back in the 1970's and 1980's, before political correctness and threats of terrorism, the sales presentations were more exciting than they were in later years. Back then, students could bring just about anything into the building for a sales presentation and nobody gave it a second thought. I recall numerous students in that era selling shotguns, rifles, handguns, ammunition, crossbows, hunting knives, and everything short of a bazooka. And even that wouldn't have been off limits. In the 1990's and 2000's, students were relegated to selling toasters, socks, candles, and other boring stuff. I wonder what they'll be selling in another ten or twenty years.

My friend who taught Speech said that his job amounted to listening to boring speech after boring speech after boring speech. Occasionally, though, there would be a speech or a demonstration that would be so exciting, unusual, entertaining, wild, or off the wall that it made up for the hours of boredom.

The speech teacher had emphasized the importance of having an opening statement that is a real grabber and that will capture the immediate, relevant, complete attention of the listener. One female student, about thirty years old, understood his point and put it into action when she started her speech by saying, "I'm going to die from AIDS – my husband has screwed every stripper within a hundred miles." I suspect that adequately got everyone's attention.

One of his most memorable demonstration speeches started out silently. A young man walked to the front of the room carrying a large box that was obviously very heavy. He sat the box down on the table and pulled out an electric cord about eight feet long. The cord had two strands and he proceeded to pull them apart on the end opposite the plug-in. Next, he took a knife and bared the ends of the wires, removing about two inches of the rubber casing. He then reached into the box and removed some kind of homemade crate and placed it on the table. Next, he removed a live pig from the box, placed it on the crate, and tied the pig down so it couldn't escape. Then, he stuck one of the bare wires into the pig's butt and put the other one in the pig's mouth, plugged in the wire, and electrocuted the pig in front of the whole class.

No one knew what his point was, perhaps other than to add some shock value to his demonstration, and he didn't get a chance to explain. Half of the class gasped in horror, while others screamed, and several cried. Meanwhile, the smell of scorched pig was starting to waft throughout the room and students held their noses as they ran for the door.

One of the measuring sticks of a good demonstration is whether or not it has staying power. That is, was it a demonstration that someone might remember the next day or the next or the next or even maybe next month. It's safe to say that the demonstration with the pig had oodles of staying power, if nothing else.

Sue 'Em

I taught the Real Estate Principles course where the enrollment was about evenly divided between students from the Small Business Management Program and the Legal Assistant Program. This made for a very interesting mix.

Over half of the students in the Legal Assistant program were *non-traditional* students, having graduated from high school some six to ten years ago, or more. The non-traditional students were paying their own money to go to college and they also valued their time. Therefore, they were extremely conscientious, serious-minded students who rarely missed class, studied hard, were always prepared, and wanted to learn all that they could. The attitude and work ethic of these non-traditional students rubbed off on the younger students in the program and they, too, were dedicated students.

The students in the Legal Assistant Program were studying to be paralegals, which means that upon graduation, they would be hired by a lawyer to assist them with legal research, preparing legal briefs, and similar matters. In fact, the Legal Assistant students seemed to view themselves as *mini lawyers*, and therein, often, was the root of the situation.

The Legal Assistant students analyzed every word that was spoken or written in class, always looking for a loophole that they could argue about. And, when we studied any situation that resulted in a controversy between two parties, they always had the same solution – well, let me give you an example.

A case for discussion in the real estate textbook said, "You own a vacant lot in a new resort development about a hundred miles from your home where you plan to build a cottage some day. You bought the bare lot two years ago when the development was brand new. Since then, a few new houses have been built in the subdivision. Because the lot is a hundred miles from your home and since it is bare land that requires no constant attention, you only stop to check on your lot about once a year when you're in the area anyway. Yesterday, you stopped to check on your lot and were shocked at what you discovered. Your next-door neighbor, who bought a bare lot at about the same time you did, is starting to build a home on his lot. So far, the contractor has only dug a hole in the ground for the basement, but the problem is that the hole is about three feet over the lot line onto your property. What should you do?"

Without hesitation, the Legal Assistant students would shout, "Sue 'em," "Take him to court," "Sue the guilty S.O.B," "Take him for everything he's got," "Sue the dirty dog," and stuff like that. This did not surprise me, because the Legal Assistants students' answer to every situation was always, "Sue 'em."

I would then ask the Business Management students what they thought should be done to cure the problem. Invariably in a situation like this, a business student would say something like, "Well, maybe the owner of the lot should go talk to the neighbor and the contractor, point out their mistake, and give them a chance to cure the problem before any real harm is done."

Most of the Legal Assistant students had a look on their face that seemed to say, "What kind of a screwball solution is that?"

I would then ask a Legal Assistant student what they thought of that recommendation. They would normally ponder the situation for a moment and then begrudgingly admit, "Well, it might work … but if it doesn't, we'll sue the hell out of 'em."

When we would review an examination that the students had taken, the Legal Assistant students turned the discussion into a battlefield with them on one side and me on the other. In their minds, they were lawyers arguing their case and they didn't care if the answer they had on the test was wrong, they thought that they should get credit for it if they could present a strong argument to support their contention. Fortunately, I was the *Judge* and there was no appellate court. However, I could tell by the look in the eyes of the Legal Assistant students that each and every one of them was thinking, "I wonder if we can sue him."

And Then, I Remembered What You Taught Me

There is probably no one on earth as dangerous as a person who has a little bit of knowledge on a certain topic – particularly if they don't realize that their knowledge level is little. I sometimes wondered what my former students did out there in the world with the knowledge that they had learned from me in the courses that I taught. Oh, I'm sure that most of the "A" and "B" students realized what they knew and what they didn't know and normally didn't try to exceed their level of understanding. Mostly, it was the "D" students that I worried about – the ones that had a flirting acquaintance with the subject matter, but who might think that they knew more than they actually did, or might confuse what they knew with what they didn't know in a jumbled mess.

I recall a student named Russell, who took both the Business Law and Real Estate Principles courses from me – a dangerous double whammy. In class, whenever Russell would volunteer an answer to a question, he would start out in one direction and before he was done with his answer, he'd end up going in the opposite direction, thus answering the question and contradicting his own answer at the same time. It was impossible to decipher whether his final answer was "Yes,"

"No," "Maybe," or "I don't know."

About three years after Russell completed his studies, he stopped in to see me to thank me for all that I had taught him in the Business Law and Real Estate courses. He said that he had recently had a controversy with his landlord and he described the situation to me in detail. The landlord and he had totally opposite points of view in the matter. Russell said that he had convinced the landlord to change his mind, though, when he told him, "I studied Business Law and Real Estate Principles and Professor David Peterson taught me…" And then Russell quoted back to me the magical words that I had said in class that allowed him to win his argument – except that Russell had everything totally backwards and absolutely wrong.

It is said that the way in which a message is delivered is often more important than the message itself. In this case, Russell apparently delivered the message with such confidence and force that the landlord actually thought that he knew what he was talking about. Who knows, maybe the landlord had been a student of mine, too.

I wonder how many Russell's I have turned loose on an unsuspecting world. Judging from the number of students who earned "D's" from me, it could be in the hundreds.

If you ever get involved in an argument or controversy with someone who confidently quotes facts, figures, procedures or rules in an attempt to win the argument, you might ask them, "Did you ever take a course from Professor David Peterson?"

Quotable Quotes

They say that kids say the darnedest things. The same could be said of students. I wish when I started teaching, I would have realized that one day I would write this book. I would have carefully recorded every quotable quote uttered by students through the years, which could have undoubtedly filled an entire book by itself. But, I do recall a few memorable gems.

I once kept track of the first word uttered by students when they entered my office or stopped me in the hallway to ask a question, to make a request, or to say something. The first word, or should I say *sound*, uttered by over ninety-five percent of the students was, "Uh." As in, "Uh, do we have class today?" "Uh, I won't be in class tomorrow." "Uh, I didn't get my assignment done," or "Uh, I Uh, Uh, I Uh, can't remember what I was going to ask you."

ooooo

At the end of the semester, one student offered a philosophical quote that has puzzled me for around twenty years. He said, "I may be getting a "D," but I learned a lot more than the "A" students."

The statement so confounded me that I failed to ask him for an explanation. But what I think he might have meant was that the "A" students already knew most of that stuff when the class began so they gained very little additional knowledge. He, on the other hand, knew absolutely nothing when the class started and he worked himself all the way up to a "D." Ya, you're probably right – I don't have a clue to what he meant.

○○○○○

I taught the state Real Estate Pre-License Course for persons who wanted to enter the real estate profession. The course was mandatory before a person could sit for the state exam. Upon passing the exam, they would work under a real estate broker as a salesperson.

Typically, when a person became a salesperson, their broker would inform the local newspaper, and a reporter would interview the salesperson – free publicity for the broker and the salesperson. The reporter would ask various questions, but one that could always be counted on was, "Why did you enter the real estate business?" I informed the students in the Pre-License Course that this interview would take place and that this particular question would be asked and suggested that they give some thought to it so they could give a dynamite answer.

One of my students, John, passed the state exam, was hired by a broker, was interviewed by a reporter and, was asked *the question*. His answer was, "I entered the real estate profession because I want to help people."

I had several reactions to his answer: First, John evidently took my advice and prepared an answer for the reporter. Second, what a great answer. Third, what a bunch of bullshit.

If John really wanted to help people, he should have gone into the ministry or become a social worker or teacher. But, I was proud of John; he said the politically correct thing to say, and there was no doubt in my mind, that with a line like that, he was going to become a howling success in the real estate business.

∞∞∞

I was teaching a college course in Real Estate Principles and posed this question to the students: "A homeowner lists his home for sale with a real estate agent. When the house sells, the homeowner is to pay the real estate agent a sales commission of seven percent (7%) of the sales price. The homeowner wants to net $100,000 for himself after paying the real estate commission. At what price must the home sell in order for the owner to net $100,000?"

The students crunched some numbers for a few minutes. I asked students for their answers, which ranged from $93,000 to $120,000 with just about everything in between. I should note that the calculation is actually trickier and more difficult than it first appears.

I proceeded to work through the calculation, writing the step-by-step procedure and the correct answer on the board. I had my back to the students and had just finished writing the answer when I heard a female voice, loud and clear say, "Where the F*** did he get that number?" This was followed by the sound of a book being slammed shut and of high heels pounding the floor on the way to the door.

I turned around and I suspect that my mouth was hanging open. One of her classmates said, "That's just Sally – she does that all the time."

By the way, you might want to try to calculate the answer to the question yourself. The correct answer is $107,526.88. Did you get that number, or would you be inclined to say, well, what Sally said?"

⁂

Some genius at our college got to thinking about all of the Vietnam veterans that were in the community and about how each of them was entitled to veteran's education benefits. Most of these guys were in their thirties, had full-time jobs and families, and weren't about to quit their jobs to go back to college full-time just to claim their GI benefits. But, this genius devised a plan where we could offer a night school program that would allow the veterans to go to college full-time and thus earn their full veteran's educational pay.

The program was identified by the acronym, ADVANCE, which stood for some long name that no one knew, except that the letter, V, most likely stood for *Veteran*.

The students in the ADVANCE program took two classes on Tuesday night and two classes on Thursday night, which made them a full-time student, which earned them their full veteran's education cash payment. Each night, the first class went from 6 p.m. – 9 p.m. and the second class went from 9 p.m. to midnight.

Some of the veterans in the program figured that as long as they were there anyway, they'd try their best to learn all that they could, and they took it very seriously. Most of them, however, openly admitted that the program amounted to nothing more than a part-time job and that they were there only for the money.

The ADVANCE program was wildly successful and virtually every veteran in the area signed up. The veterans got their veteran's education pay, the college got its tuition and sold some books, and the faculty earned extra money by teaching one or two extra classes a week.

I taught one of the first ADVANCE courses ever offered, which was taken by about fifty veterans from my community. I knew about two-thirds of the students personally.

It was somewhat of an unwritten rule that no ADVANCE student would be given an "F" unless there was no way around it. However, since some of the students hadn't put much effort into the class, they would undoubtedly receive a "D" as a final grade.

On the final night of class I addressed this issue with them saying, "Some of you are friends and neighbors and acquaintances of mine and I hope you realize that I have to do my job now and must give you a grade for this course. I hope you realize that if the grade isn't as high as you'd like it to be, it's just the way the scores came out on the grading scale and its nothing personal and . . . .

One of the veterans in the back row interrupted me

and yelled, "Don't worry about it, they pay the "D's" just like they pay the "A's." The roar of laughter confirmed that they understood what I had to do and that it was okay. And, as long as the check cleared the bank, they were happy.

A Tender Side

It was fun to recall the goofy and humorous incidents involving students and to share those memories with you. One of my most vivid memories of students, however, occurred at a very sad time in my life.

In the mid 1990's, my mother passed away. I missed about a week of classes to attend the funeral and to take care of various details.

My students had all been informed of the reason for my absence. When I returned, numerous students, some of whom I barely knew, stopped me in the hallway, came into my office, or stopped after class to offer their condolences.

The students in the Small Business Management Program took numerous courses that I taught and by the time that they graduated, we got to know each other quite well. They gave me a lovely card, signed by everyone in the program.

The students in the Legal Assistant Program took two courses that I taught. They were serious, dedicated students who would argue with me over anything and everything, it would seem, just to prove a point or to gain an extra point on an exam they had taken. After class that first day I was back, however, I saw a different side of the Legal Assistant students. They presented me with a beautiful card, signed by each of them, and offered me warm and sincere best wishes. The Legal Assistant students have a special place in my heart, for being dedicated, serious students who had enough gumption to fight for what they believed in and because of the special kindness that they showed me at that sad and difficult time.

Tests And Grading

"I will do *anything* for an "A," she said.

"Try studying," I replied.

Even though the course subject matter, class attendance, daily assignments, and gaining knowledge were often of little interest to students, grades were. Many of them would go to great lengths to get a good grade including cheating on tests, plagiarizing term papers, lying about reasons for class absences, and *anything*. Some students even resorted to studying.

I often asked groups of students what they expected to get out of going to college. Almost all of their responses fell into these categories: "Good grades," "A college degree," "Knowledge," or "A good job."

While on the surface those responses might seem to be good answers to the question, each of them is only partially correct – they all need to be tied together. Why does a person go to college? Well, the ultimate reason is the expectation that it will lead to having a good life, which is the result of having a fulfilling and good-paying job, which is the result of getting their degree, which is the result of getting good grades, which is the result of gaining enough knowledge to get those grades. Think about it for a moment.

Giving Exams

I looked forward to giving exams to my students. It was a nice break from the daily lectures and discussions and it gave me feedback on how my students were doing in the course, and maybe how I was doing as the teacher as well.

I always checked the exams the same day that I gave them and handed them back to students the next time that class met so we could discuss them. My main goal in discussing the exam with students after they had taken it was the hope that they would learn things through the discussion that they obviously didn't know when they took the exam. The students' main goal in discussing the exam was to try to gain extra points on the exam by arguing that their wrong answer should be considered correct because the wording was misleading or for some other reason.

During my first year of teaching, I was scrambling with preparing for five different classes and meeting all the other demands of the job, so I usually gave the standard exams that were provided for the course by the textbook publisher. Often, the questions were poorly written and I would end up trying to defend an answer that maybe even I didn't agree with, or I'd end up granting the students credit for numerous wrong answers.

After suffering through the better part of my first year of teaching using the standard textbook exams, I wrote all of my own exams for the remaining years of my teaching career. At least then I knew what I had in mind when I wrote the question and was in a better position to defend my answer.

I enjoyed the mental gymnastics of debating the exam with the students, of defending the exam's answers, and of deflecting the students' contentions of why a wrong answer should be considered right, while trying to be fair to the students at the same time. And I enjoyed the challenge of occasionally trying to convince them that my wrong answer actually was right.

World-Class Cheaters

It is my belief that most students I had in class did not attempt to cheat on exams. For one thing, I'm sure they figured there would be hell to pay if I caught them. They most likely knew that I would not simply kick them out of class, but would keep them around the entire semester so I could torture them and would then end up flunking them anyway.

Everyone knows about the ordinary ways of cheating on an exam – writing notes on your hand, turning the pages of the book with your feet, palming a crib sheet with teeny-weeny lettering, sneaking a peek at a neighbor's answer sheet, and whispering to your neighbor. A couple of students took cheating on an exam to a higher level, or at least they tried to, and I'd like to tell you about them.

Leonard, The Amazing Accountant

I was teaching a course in Accounting Principles that met at 9 a.m. on Monday, Wednesday, and Friday. I arrived at my office about fifteen minutes ahead of class time on Monday and immediately noticed that there were paper particles on top of a stack of papers on the floor next to the wall. It appeared that a mouse might have been in my office over the weekend. Since I didn't have time to do further inspection myself, I called my friend, Bob, who was a custodian and asked him if he'd check it out to see if there was any sign of a mouse and if so, if he'd set a mousetrap.

I had scheduled an Accounting exam for that Monday morning, so I grabbed the test papers and headed for class. After the exam, I returned to my office and found a note from Bob saying that he had done a thorough inspection of my office and was sure that there was no mouse, and, in fact did not find any evidence other than the paper particles that one had been there at all.

I had the following hour free, so I set about checking the Accounting exams. There were four pages to the exam and I checked page one on everyone's test first, then checked page two on everyone's exam, then checked page three on everyone's exam, and finally checked page four on everyone's exam. Since the four pages were stapled together, most students just put their name on the first page, so as I checked pages 2, 3, and 4, I had no idea who was getting the questions all right or who was missing them all until I went back and added up the check marks on each test. It was always an interesting time to see who had scored what on the exam.

I went through each test paper, adding up the number of points they got on each page and writing their final score on the first page. There were 100 points in the exam. Mary got 87, John got 79, Marjo got 94, Bill got 66, Amanda got

83, Leonard got 96, Shirley got…Whoa!

Leonard got 96? Leonard? Absolutely impossible! This was the third exam of the course and Leonard had scored 58 and 46 on his first two exams. He had missed class several times since, had turned in no assignments, and had slept through most of the classes that he did attend since the last exam. Either there had been divine intervention from above, way above, on Leonard's behalf, or Leonard had cheated on the exam. I chose to believe the latter; in fact, I was sure of it – but how?

I had watched all of the students carefully during the exam, including Leonard, and I just knew that there was no way he could have cheated. I recalled observing Leonard working diligently on the test. Never once did his eyes wander to another student's paper, never once did he whisper to another student or pass a paper back and forth with another student. I knew he had cheated, but how?

I was sitting in my chair behind my desk staring at the wall, trying to figure out how Leonard could have cheated on the exam. My eyes focused on four smudges on the wall; each was a streak about a half-inch wide, a quarter inch apart and six inches long. Funny I had never noticed them before, but then, if someone asked me what color the walls in my kitchen at home were, I probably couldn't tell them that, either. Then I noticed a bigger, wider black smudge on the wall just above the stack of papers with the mysterious paper particles on the top.

My gaze drifted to the ceiling directly above the stack of

papers. There was a suspended ceiling in my office, consisting of two foot by two foot ceiling panels made of some type of particleboard that rested on metal frames. The panel directly above the stack of papers on the floor was askew – the one side did not fit cleanly and fully onto the metal frame. Strange that I had never noticed that either…

It all came to me in a flash – I knew exactly how Leonard had cheated on the exam.

Over the weekend, Leonard had gotten into the building, which would have been easy to do. There was a reception area about sixteen feet long between my office and the hallway. Apparently, Leonard had helped himself to a ladder from the custodian's workroom, had climbed up on it, and had pushed up a ceiling panel in the hallway. From there, he would have been able to climb up on the concrete block wall that ran along the reception area and straight to my office. Since it is at least ten feet from the top of the block wall to the building's roof, Leonard could walk upright along the block wall.

When he got to my office, Leonard pulled up a ceiling panel and lowered himself into my office. Since the stack of papers was on the floor along the wall, he had to push off from the wall to avoid landing on them, thus explaining the four smudged streaks caused by his fingers and the broader smudge above the stack of papers where his foot pushed off. The paper particles on top of the stack of papers were actually pieces of the ceiling panel that scraped off when Leonard pulled it up from the metal frame. Then, he had stood on top of my desk to replace the ceiling panel, but couldn't get it to fit all the way down in the metal frame – the fatal flaw in his plan.

On the previous Friday afternoon, I had placed the Accounting exam on the shelf behind my chair so it would be ready to go on Monday morning. Leonard would have been able to locate it with ease and he must have laughed out loud when he saw my answer key lying on top of the stack of test papers.

Leonard then sat down in my chair at my desk and copied the answers from my answer key onto one of the blank test papers, missing a couple of answers on purpose. He then put the answer key back where it belonged, put my chair back where it had been, and walked out of my office, through the reception area, and out into the hallway, with the exam in his hand. It should be noted that the office doors were locked from the outside but could be opened from the inside.

During the test, Leonard had put on a good show, diligently working on the test paper I had distributed to him and then, when I wasn't looking, he switched it with the one he had made in my office and handed that one in.

And, that is exactly how Leonard did it. Now, what to do about it.

I toyed with several different scenarios of how I would confront Leonard but realized that an out and out confrontation probably wouldn't work. He would simply deny that he had done it and I had no actual proof. It would be his word against my suspicions.

Then, in an instant, I experienced that phenomenon known as the *creative leap*, whereby the solution was suddenly delivered to me, totally and perfectly. I laughed out loud as though suddenly possessed by a demon. Now, if I could only pull it off.

I walked into class on Wednesday morning with the exams in my hand. I looked straight at Leonard and said, "Leonard, will you come with me, please."

Leonard followed me out the door and we walked in silence to my office. I motioned for Leonard to take a seat and I closed the door. Leonard looked mystified – what could I possibly want to talk to him about?

"Leonard," I said, "I want to talk to you about Monday's Accounting exam." I hesitated for a moment hoping that maybe he would crack and confess. He didn't even flinch.

"Are you sure that you turned in your exam?" I asked.

"What do you mean?" he said slowly, apparently getting a little suspicious.

"I mean you didn't turn in your scratch paper and throw your test paper in the wastebasket or put your test paper in your backpack by accident, did you?" I asked.

"I know I turned my paper in and I know I had my name on it too," he said. "What's going on?"

"Well, I was pretty sure that you had turned in your test paper, too," I said. "In fact, I remember you doing so. And you might find this as hard to believe as I do, but someone broke into my office last night, Leonard, and the only thing that seems to be missing is *your* exam."

Leonard turned pale. I could imagine him wanting to scream, "It was Saturday when I broke into your office, you idiot, not last night" but, of course, he couldn't, could he!

"Apparently he got hold of a ladder, probably from the custodian's workroom," I continued. "He climbed up on the ladder out in the hallway, lifted up a ceiling panel, climbed up onto the block wall, and walked along it until he came to my office. Then he pulled up that ceiling tile," I said, pointing to the one that was slightly askew, "and lowered himself into my office. You can see where he pushed off the wall there with his hand and there with his foot to avoid landing on that stack of papers on the floor," I said, again pointing to the evidence. I intentionally referred to the intruder as *he* to insinuate that I knew everything.

"See those particles on the top of the pile of papers?" I asked. "Well, those came from when he lifted up the ceiling panel."

Leonard looked like someone had hit him in the face with a shovel. The fight had been taken out of him.

"Leonard, I do need an exam from you, so I'll have to ask you to take the test again, right now. You'll still remember most of what you knew on Monday," I said.

I led Leonard to the empty desk in the reception area and handed him the exam. "If you have any questions, you can ask one of my colleagues here," I said, pointing to two of the business teachers sitting in their offices, who were in on the ruse and who had been recruited to keep a watchful eye on Leonard when he retook the exam.

As I was about to leave the reception area and head back to my Accounting class, I stopped and said, "Oh, by the way, since the only thing missing was your exam, I'll let you decide if we should notify the police and have them conduct an investigation of the break-in." It was fun to twist the knife a little bit.

"N-No," Leonard said. "I'll just take the test over."

I smiled at Leonard - that smile that says "I gottcha. I gottcha and there's not a damn thing you can do about it." And he knew that I was right.

By the way, Leonard scored 44 on the exam the second time around. He withdrew from the course a week later and I never saw him again. But, I never forgot him and never forgot the opportunity that he gave me to enjoy one of my fondest moments as a teacher.

Cool Conrad

Conrad was a hot dog. He made no bones about the fact that his dad owned some factory and that he was on the factory payroll and received a monthly check, although he hadn't set foot inside the factory for many months. He had flunked out of or had been kicked out of several colleges and universities around the country and his dad had hauled him back home to the area community college as a last-ditch attempt to get Conrad educated.

Conrad prided himself on the fact that he never bought a textbook for any of his courses, never took any notes in class, missed class often, and was still able to pass the course. Well, that was the type of thinking that apparently got him flunked out of or kicked out of those other colleges. Word was around the faculty that you had to watch Conrad like a hawk during a test because he would use every cheating method known to mankind.

Conrad was a student of mine in the era before computers were widely used. We in the Business Department had an office complex with several individual offices around the outside of a reception area. There was a desk in the reception area that had an IBM typewriter that most of us used to type our tests, since it made sharp copies that could be easily duplicated. The typewriter used a one-time-use film ribbon that wound from a spool on the right of the machine to a spool on the left of the machine after it had been typed on. Therefore, every character that was typed left an impression on the film ribbon that wound onto the spool on the left. The film ribbon was extremely thin and over a hundred yards of film was contained on a single spool.

Conrad noticed that I often used that typewriter with the film ribbon. Several days before a scheduled exam, he started to hang around our office a little more than normal. One day I was typing something and Conrad, who considered himself to be pretty smooth and to be quite a charmer, asked, "Typing our Business Law test?"

"Yes I am," I replied.

The next day when our office secretary sat down at the typewriter, the film ribbon was missing. I knew instantly what had happened – Conrad. I smiled to myself. Although the film ribbon contained every letter of every word that had been typed, the machine didn't place the letters in order, it scrambled them, obviously to thwart someone from doing what Conrad was attempting to do. Besides that, I was *not* typing the Business Law exam like I told Conrad; I was typing a memo to my boss.

I smiled to myself as I pictured the image of Conrad unwinding yard after yard of the black film ribbon, searching for the spot where I had typed the exam, and trying to unscramble the letters and words on the ribbon.

Conrad showed up for the exam the following day. As I passed out the exams, I took special note of Conrad's fingernails, the tips of which were black as coal.

"Your fingernails look like you've been playing in the dirt," I said to Conrad.

He looked up at me and I could see a wave of understanding wash over him. He didn't say a word, but I could tell he was thinking, "You dirty dog – you set me up."

Well, I didn't set Conrad up; he did it to himself, although I happily helped guide him in the right direction a little bit.

Predictably, Conrad flunked my exam, flunked the course, and flunked his other courses as well. I never saw him after that semester. I wonder if he's still on the factory payroll.

A Way With Words

One of my colleagues, Professor Williams, assigned two major term papers, one due at mid-term and the other due at the end of the semester. Each counted one-fourth of the final grade of the course.

You've, no doubt, had this feeling yourself from time to time where things just don't look right. Well, that's the feeling that Professor Williams had when he graded Robert's midterm paper. The problem was that it was a near masterpiece. It was well researched and well written and contained great insight into the topic. That, coupled with the fact that Robert had great difficulty constructing even a basic sentence, either verbally or in writing, and that Robert had shown little comprehension of the course's subject matter made Professor Williams suspicious. Oh, and Robert was dating one of the smartest girls on campus.

When Robert turned in his term paper at the end of the semester, the Professor grabbed it and turned it face down on his desk. "What's the title of your paper?" he asked Robert.

Robert turned pale. "What?" he asked.

"What's the title of your term paper?" Professor Williams repeated.

"I, uh, well, uh, it's uh, well, uh," Robert stammered.

"Tell me the title of your term paper and I'll give you a final grade of "A" for the course," Professor Williams challenged.

"Uh, uh, uh," Robert moaned as his face turned a whiter shade of pale.

Busted.

Mysterious Fall From Grace

Sandra had been the top student in my class the entire semester. She had scored the top paper on each of the three exams during the semester and was the one person who I could always call on for an answer if the rest of the students failed me. She always attended class, was always prepared, and was always pleasant.

I gave the final exam as scheduled, two days before the end of the semester. It was a multiple-choice exam where the students marked their answers on an answer sheet rather than on the test paper itself.

I was always anxious to see how the students would do on their final. There were always a few who did better on the exam than I anticipated and always a few who didn't fare as well as I expected. When I got to Sandra's exam, though, I was floored. My top student, who had averaged 96 on the three previous exams, scored 58 on this one. Something was drastically wrong.

I immediately assumed that I had messed something up which caused Sandra's score to be so low. Had I given her a different version of the test somehow, so her answers didn't match those on my answer key? Had the pages of the exam that I gave her been assembled in the wrong order, thus throwing off all of her answers on the answer sheet? Or had she made a mistake by skipping a question somewhere that caused her answers to be off by one or two lines on the answer sheet? I didn't know what had happened but it appeared obvious to me that something had gone terribly wrong.

Sandra had been my top student all semester long and I simply assumed that she would score well on the final and get her "A" for the course. I graded on the total point basis and if

I used the score of 58 for her final exam, she would get a final grade of "C."

I decided that I needed to talk to Sandra to see if she could help explain what had happened. I obtained her phone number from her records in the Registrar's office and left a message on her answering machine to call me.

About an hour later, Sandra called. Before I could explain why I wanted to talk to her, Sandra blurted out, "Ya, I know, I bombed the final. I was having trouble in another class and needed to study hard for that exam and didn't have time to study for yours."

"I just wanted to talk to you and make sure you knew that the final hadn't gone well," I said, "so when final grades come out you'll know why you got the grade that you got."

"I know," she said.

I was shocked. My top student all semester long wasn't a top student after all. She was simply able to cram for a test and to remember the information just long enough to score well on the exam, and then she apparently forgot everything the moment she walked out the door.

A procedure that I have tried to follow throughout my life, when there is a controversy or problem, is to let the other person talk first. Often, I have found, they will reveal information that is helpful to me or will save me from making a fool of myself by demonstrating that there really wasn't a controversy or problem at all.

If Sandra had simply let me talk first, I would have explained to her that something, somehow had gone wrong with the test that I gave her and that I was mystified as to what it was. She could have easily picked up on this and simply could have said something like, "I thought I did pretty well on the test."

If Sandra had said something like that, it would have confirmed my suspicions that I had somehow fouled up the test that I gave her and that it was my fault that she scored so low. Therefore, since it was my fault, I would have volunteered to grade her on the first three exams she took and to throw this one out, thus giving her an "A" for the course.

I had several students who were like Sandra, capable of cramming knowledge into their head to score high on a test, but incapable of remembering any of that knowledge beyond a few days. I often wondered what their employer thought when they found out that this "A" student they had just hired knew almost nothing.

Begging For A Grade

I, as well as many of my colleagues, determined final grades on the total point basis. To use this system, the teacher records in their grade book or computer the points scored by each student on each test, assignment, and other factor in determining the student's final grade. At the end of the semester, the teacher totals each student's points. The instructor also determines the minimum total points needed to earn a final grade of an "A," "B," "C," or "D."

Often, after grades come out some two or three weeks after the end of the semester, a student finds that they received a lower grade than they expected. They then go see the instructor for an explanation and, of course, to argue to have their grade raised.

The teacher whips out their grade book or computer printout and shows the student the total points that they earned and then shows them the grading scale indicating the number of points that were needed to get a particular grade. In many cases, out of maybe 800 possible points in the course, the student missed getting the grade that they thought they had earned by a measly three or four points. They argue, beg, and plead for the instructor to give them the higher grade since they were so close. But, undoubtedly the teacher holds their ground since the grade has already been listed on the student's permanent transcript.

Are the teachers being hard-hearted by refusing to give the student a break when they were that close to the higher grade that they coveted? Are the teachers being pompous, believing that their grading scale is infallible and that they simply can not lower the grading scale a point or two to give the student the benefit of the doubt and therefore the higher grade?

Usually, the teacher's being or not being hard-hearted or pompous has nothing to do with it. It is all about *the system*. At most schools and colleges, when a teacher turns in their final grades to the Principal or Registrar, they are the *final* grades. They cannot be changed by the teacher later on unless the teacher files a written appeal which includes an explanation of why the grade turned in was in error and why the grade should be changed.

Usually there are only a few reasons that are acceptable for making a grade change, such as the teacher found a student's term paper under a heap on their desk, that they had not included in the student's final point total. Furthermore, the teacher may need to argue their case and provide documentation to an Academic Review Committee before the grade can be changed. I suspect that this rule was instituted partially so that play directors, athletic coaches, music teachers, debate coaches and others can't put pressure on a teacher to change a grade to keep their star performer eligible for competition.

There is a magical time, though, when a student has the opportunity to plead their case with their instructor for a higher grade and when the instructor is in a position to easily give them that grade, if they are inclined to do so, without going through any red tape or procedures. It is a small window of opportunity, lasting only from two to seven days per grading period. That magical window of opportunity is at the end of the grading period, *after* the final exam is taken and *before* the instructor turns in the final grades, which is usually at the end of the final test week or the start of the following week.

A reason that many college students fail to take advantage of this window of opportunity to state their case and to argue for a higher grade, if they are aware of this small time frame at all, is that they are often anxious to get out of there and to go on vacation. It would be wise, after spending perhaps 45 hours sitting in class and hundreds of hours studying for the course, for a student to spend a few extra hours on campus to ensure that they get the grade that they deserve, or maybe even a grade better than they deserve.

I recall a student, Jennifer, who stopped in my office to check on her grade during that magical period between when the final exam was graded and when grades were to be turned in. It was a Business Math course and, unfortunately, no matter how hard she tried, she just couldn't get it. She had failed three of the four exams during the semester and had bombed the final. She had attended class regularly, had turned in all required assignments, and had tried hard, very hard. Still, her final point total was twenty points below the bottom "D."

Jennifer tried just about every strategy in the book to try to convince me to give her a "D" for a final grade. She thought I was a fabulous teacher (good strategy), she liked Business Math (good strategy), and she had studied hard (good strategy) but just could not figure out all of those formulas.

She explained that if she failed this course, she would not graduate (emotional strategy) and her family would be terribly disappointed (emotional strategy). They were all coming to her graduation ceremony in three days and it would be terribly embarrassing (sympathy strategy) for her if she were not included in the ceremony. Furthermore, she had a great summer job lined up and if she had to repeat the Business Math course in the summer, she would lose a bunch of money (economic strategy). She offered to do extra credit work to bring her grade up from a "F" to a "D" (compromising strategy) and then she said, "and I just don't want to be a failure," (sympathy strategy). And with that she broke down and cried (heart-wrenching emotional strategy).

I turned to my computer and began typing. When I finished, I handed Jennifer a sheet of paper with the following written on it.

AGREEMENT

I, Jennifer Anders, do hereby admit that I am absolutely horrible at performing Business Mathematical calculations. I also admit that I earned an "F" and deserved an "F" in the Business Mathematics course that I took. I hereby agree to the following, in return for having my final grade raised from the "F" that I deserved to a "D" in the Business Mathematics course:

I, Jennifer Anders, promise to never, ever, my entire life, even if I am threatened or beaten, divulge to anyone, either directly or indirectly, that I ever took a Business Mathematics course from Professor David Peterson.

Signed: _____
Jennifer Anders

Jennifer read the words on the paper very carefully and then looked up at me with hopeful eyes. "Are you serious?" she asked.

"Yes I am," I replied. "You agree to never, ever, the rest of your life, tell a soul that you took the Business Math course from me and I'll give you the "D."

She quickly signed the paper, apparently being fearful

that I was only joking or might change my mind. She handed it to me and I showed her my grade book as I crossed off her final grade of "F" and changed it to "D."

I have never seen a more grateful person in my life. I believe I did the right thing in changing her grade to the "D." It allowed her to go on with her life. Forcing her to retake the Business Math course once, twice, or ten times probably wouldn't have turned her into a business mathematician of any worth anyway. Besides, I thought that the multitude of strategies that she used to try to get me to change her grade was easily worth another twenty-five or thirty points.

I never considered my grading scale to be infallible. Therefore, if a student's point total was borderline, and if it appeared that the student was interested in the course and had given it a good effort, I often raised that borderline student's grade to the next higher grade. I'm sure that many of my students were pleasantly surprised when their grades came out and some may even have suspected that I had made an error in calculating their grade.

Many students approached me after grades came out, wondering why they didn't receive a higher grade. I do not, however, recall anyone ever asking me if I had made a mistake and gave him or her a higher grade than they deserved. Imagine that.

Students: They're Almost...

In my thirty-eight year teaching career, I came in contact with thousands of students. They ranged from brilliant to dimwitted, charismatic to dull, energetic to lethargic, serious to goofy, normal to insane, scholars to dunderheads, intellectuals to knuckleheads, dullards to party animals, and a whole lot who fell in between. They had their good points and their bad points, but each contributed something to the class and to the school, somehow, in their own way. Usually, the contribution was positive, but in some cases it was something that the school is still trying to live down or to cover up.

I sincerely believe that virtually every student that I met had the ability to pass their courses and earn a college degree. The only thing that stopped some of them was themselves - by not putting forth enough effort.

Some of my students went out into the world and became miserable flops, it is true. I try not to take the blame for this. Many of my students went out into the world and became fabulous successes. I try to take as much credit for this as I can.

I am pleased to say that many of my former students became very good personal friends of mine after they graduated. I am just as proud to say that I do not have a former student that I consider to be an enemy or that I am ashamed of.

David Peterson/Peter Davidson

If I were to summarize my feelings about students in a word or two, it would be this – they were *almost human*.

The Faculty

I taught with hundreds of teachers throughout my career and I observed them in many situations and circumstances. I saw them teaching a classroom of students, working in their offices, debating issues in faculty meetings, tutoring students, attending in-services, relaxing in the faculty lounge, preparing for classes, doing research in the library, serving on committees, advising students, attending school-related functions, participating in fund raisers, and having fun. I came to know them well.

There is an old saying that is attributed to George Bernard Shaw – *"Those who can, do. Those who can't, teach."* Like a lot of sayings, it is cute and clever – and like a lot of sayings, it is largely inaccurate.

In my opinion, the vast majority of teachers I worked with were highly competent people who were knowledgeable, talented, dedicated, hard working, and sincere. They were successful as teachers and would have been successful in another line of work also if they had chosen to pursue it. This was proven to be true many times where a successful teacher I knew left the profession to pursue another occupation and became successful there, also.

One former colleague of mine left teaching and later became vice president of one of the twelve Federal Reserve

Banks in America. Two others became Presidents of major U.S. corporations. One became the economist for a major Midwest utility. Another opened his own highly successful accounting firm and others became successful in insurance, investments, consulting, sales, and retailing.

To be honest, though, not all of the teachers that I have known were competent. Some had poor communication skills and a few didn't understand the subject matter themselves, both of which pose major handicaps for a teacher.

A couple were condescending elitists, considering themselves to be smarter and better than their stupid students and they delighted in using their superior subject matter knowledge and overpowering vocabulary to teach at a level above that which their students could possibly comprehend. A few were misfits that survived in the world of academia where being eccentric is often equated with being a genius, although this is not necessarily true.

Whether they were competent or incompetent, exciting or dull, bright or dim, hard working or lazy, driven or lackadaisical, they were an interesting, diverse, and colorful bunch. Many of my fondest memories of teaching are of the teachers themselves.

The Exhibition

He started to talk about it during the first fifteen minutes of his interview for the job and he continued to talk about it every chance he got after he was hired as a social science teacher. *It* was that he wanted to put on an exhibition in front of the grandstand during halftime of a football game. He was into yoga or karate or something like that and specifically, *it* was that he wanted to lie down on the ground and have a car drive onto him to demonstrate his mystical powers.

The College made him sign a waiver, just in case the stunt didn't work, and gave him permission to go ahead with the exhibition.

He looked magnificent in his white outfit and he received mild applause when he warmed up by doing a few kicks and thrusts and when he spun around and jumped in the air a couple of times. He called four people out of the stands to help with the first phase of the exhibition, including the Dean and the college President. He handed each of them a wood dowel about four feet long and a quarter inch in diameter and had them place the dowels at the base of his throat. Then he took a few deep breaths and grunted for them to begin. Each of them pushed on the wood dowels and they bowed up in the middle until they snapped. First he bowed to his four assistants and then he turned to the grandstand, revealed his unharmed throat, and bowed. The mystical powers were working. He received moderately enthusiastic applause.

A small ramp was carried out by four assistants and placed on the ground in front of the grandstand and a car was driven up onto the ramp. It was a small car, but nevertheless, it qualified as a car. He lay down on the ground next to the ramp; his chest was the same height as the edge of the ramp. The car was eased up to the edge of the ramp. He took a series of deep breaths, "Whew, whew, whew, whew, whew."

Finally, he was ready and he grunted for the car to be driven off the ramp and onto him. He took one final deep breath and held it. The front wheels of the car were slowly driven off of the ramp and came to rest totally on him.

As soon as the wheels came to rest on him, those standing near him to provide assistance if needed, heard him groan through clenched teeth, "Get the car off."

He was never quite right after that.

A Wedding To Remember

I was a teacher through some interesting times, starting as a high school teacher in the 1960's and teaching at Lakes Community College in the 70's, 80's, 90's, and into the 2000's. I saw male students go through haircut phases from hair that hung down to their butts in the '60's to the bald dome look of the '90's. I saw female students' dress hemlines go up and down and up again, speaking of fashion trends.

The students weren't the only ones caught up in the trends of the times; we in the faculty were right there, too, although perhaps our actions were not as pronounced as those of the student body. I recall that in the late'60's and early '70's my hair covered my ears for several years and I had this great pair of shiny black and white patent leather shoes with one-inch soles and two-inch heels that I loved to wear along with black and white checkered pants and a bright red shirt. I was really something.

Somewhere during that hippie-influenced era of the 1970's one of the instructors at our college asked me if I would do him a favor at his home, which was about fifteen miles from campus. It was summertime and there were only a half dozen of us who were on duty. He had already recruited two others to help him out - one was a social science teacher who was also a minister, and the other was my friend, Dan, who taught physical education and recreation.

Songwriting has been my hobby, and aspiration, since I was about twenty-one years old. I have written over a hundred songs and a couple have been published and recorded. One was even used in a television series in The Netherlands. As an aspiring songwriter, I am always on the lookout for great stories or unusual stories that will serve as the inspiration for a song. Instead of telling you the story about what happened that day back in the '70's, in paragraph after paragraph of narrative, I summarized it in the following song lyrics.

Please notice that the last line of the chorus changes each time, as the story evolves; make sure you read all the way to the end. And, you can hum along, if you like.

A Wedding To Remember
By David R. Peterson

(For a male singer.)

Verse: They planned to get married that Tuesday afternoon
               Around noon my friend, Dan, and I were approached by the groom
               He said the attendants got mixed up on their days
               And he asked if we would step in and take their place
               Now, we didn't know the bride and groom all that well
               But figured we'd pitch in and help out, what the hell
               Now, I should explain this was back in the nineteen seventies

	And things were done differently back then, believe you me
Verse:	Now, the preacher wanted to edit the wedding vows, you see
	So he rode to the wedding with my friend, Dan, and me
	Besides the bride and groom there was only us three
	The preacher, my friend, Dan, and of course there was me
	The preacher lined us all up in the living room
	And placed my friend, Dan, right next to the groom
	The preacher made it short and got right to the point
	And in three minutes we were all headed to the nearest beer joint
Chorus:	It was a wedding to remember, ya it was quite a hoot
	The bride had on Levis and wore combat boots
	Besides the bride and groom there was only us three
	The preacher, Dan the Best Man, and then there was me
Bridge:	It was one helluva wedding reception 'till the bride and groom went on home
	Which left the preacher, Dan the Best Man, and me to carry on
	We toasted the bride and we toasted the groom
	And prayed the marriage would last at least till they got home
Chorus:	It was a wedding to remember, ya it was quite a hoot
	The bride had on Levis and wore combat boots
	Besides the bride and groom there was only us three
	The preacher, Dan the Best Man, and the Maid of Honor, hee, hee, hee
Chorus:	It was a wedding to remember, ya it was quite a hoot
	The bride had on Levis and wore combat boots
	Besides the bride and groom there was only us three
	The preacher, Dan the Best Man and the Maid of Honor – ya, that was me
Tag:	But remember, I explained this was back in the nineteen seventies
	And things were done differently back then, believe you me

Reprinted with permission, Seven Alarm Music, Inc., BMI

Well, you can see why I took up writing books. But, I

have had great fun through the years telling the story about how I, David Peterson, was the Maid of Honor in a wedding. And, that's exactly the way it happened.

Mathematical Wizardry

Professor Higgins was blazing away in front of thirty-five eager minds, listing on the board the step-by-step process for solving the mathematical brain teaser that he assigned for the day's class.

He was on Step Eight when he sneaked a peek at his work and noticed what he wrote down for Step Five. He muttered under his breath, "Oh shit."

Professor Higgins had a choice to make. On one hand, he could say something like, "Class, in reviewing my work, I see that I made an error in Step Five, which will compound itself through all of the remaining steps in solving this problem. Let me go back and start over – and I hope that I did not confuse you too badly."

On the other hand, the following thought formulated in Professor Higgins' mind, "I'm in too deep to turn back now and I'm sure as hell not going to admit that I'm capable of making an error. I'll give 'em a snow job that they'll never forget."

Professor Higgins continued to write feverishly on the board and when he was finished he read his step-by-step calculations to the class. "The inversion of the algorithm of the sine of number four divided by the congruent polynominal tangent of the number fourteen multiplied by the random variable of the number seven, when divided by the square root of zero, results in the permutation of the quadrilateral function of the sum of the subtrahend and the minuend divided by their inversion, added to the concentric isometry of the free radical number thirty-two, which results in, as you can readily see, the answer - *Three*."

"Any questions?"

The Halftime Speech

The basketball coach was always on the lookout for new ways to inspire his team. Sometimes a fiery speech was enough to do the trick. Other times, he needed a gimmick. There was the time that the team was lackluster during the first half and the coach knew that he'd need something special at halftime to jolt them out of their funk. Shortly before halftime, he instructed his student manager to find a large metal garbage can and to position it strategically in the locker room.

During halftime, the coach yelled and screamed at the team and gave them a fiery speech. As a final touch, just before the team was to return to the floor for the second half, the coach yelled, "Now get the hell out there and do something!" And then he swung his leg around and kicked the metal garbage can that the student manager had positioned off to his left. The garbage can banged into the metal lockers and made a sound like a bomb going off.

The team charged onto the floor and was so inspired by the coach's halftime show that they won the game by twenty-five points.

A dozen games later that season, the team was having another lethargic first half. The coach knew that he had to pull another rabbit out of the hat at halftime. He couldn't use the garbage can routine since he'd already done that. Then a great new idea hit him. He instructed his student manager to make arrangements.

During halftime, the coach gave one of his patented fire and brimstone speeches. To top it off, he wheeled around and swung his leg as hard as he could. He had instructed the student manager to remove the pins from the door hinges so that he could kick the door right off, which was sure to inspire the team to new heights. Unfortunately, the coach had positioned himself a little too far back. When he swung his leg around, instead of hitting the door on the side and knocking it off the hinges, he caught the door straight on. The team had heard him yell before, but nothing like this. Even though the gimmick hadn't worked out exactly as planned, it inspired the team to charge out onto the floor in a frenzy.

The coach thought that he had broken his foot and couldn't put any weight on it, so he had to kind of slide it in front of himself as he hopped onto the floor on his good foot.

Even though the gimmick backfired, the strategy worked and the team won another one in a second-half blowout.

When you have already put on the show of the century, there's not much you can do for an encore. The coach had to wait three years until there was a new crop of players who had not seen the performance. And then, it was Showtime once again.

Steven Marcus Becker

Towards the end of August, our Accounting professor suddenly resigned and left town. With only two weeks until fall classes began, that put us in quite a bind. There was no time to advertise the position in professional journals or magazines and there was barely time to place an ad in some of the larger city newspapers and to contact some of the placement services at various universities.

We realized that most business teachers had already found jobs for the new school year, but we hoped to find someone who had left teaching to enter business and who was interested in returning to teaching. Or maybe we could find an accountant who wanted to try their hand at teaching.

There was only one applicant for the job – a guy named Steven Marcus Becker who had been an accountant for an auto dealership somewhere in the middle of South Dakota. He met with the Dean on the Saturday before classes were to begin and the Dean hired him on the spot. Steven Marcus Becker apparently had been assured on the phone prior to the interview that the job was his if he wanted it since he had brought all of his worldly possessions along to the interview in a U-Haul trailer. He moved into a mobile home on Sunday and reported for work on Monday.

The rest of us in the Business Department were delighted that he was on board, since otherwise we would have had to pitch in and teach an overload until an Accounting teacher was found.

Steven Marcus Becker was a big guy with a wide smile,

long shaggy hair, penetrating eyes, and a slight limp. He insisted on being called *Marcus*. He never explained why, but I suspected it was because Marcus sounds more professorial or profound or mysterious or sophisticated than Steven.

Marcus had a mesmerizing speaking style. When he spoke, he usually leaned back in his chair with his hands clasped in front of his belly and looked wistfully off into the distance as he delivered profound knowledge like a true college professor. I had taught for almost fifteen years and had never mastered that professorial presentation style as well as Steven Marcus Becker had on his first day on the job.

Marcus had been everywhere and had done everything. He had studied law in Australia and was within a few months of his law degree when they booted him out of school for some reason that Marcus left unexplained, although he said his expulsion was truly deserved. He had almost become a doctor, but had left medical school a few months before completing his studies, again for some unexplained reason. He had been a businessman, an accountant, a martial arts instructor, a concert pianist, and several other big-time things that I cannot recall. He had read the college's ad for an Accounting instructor and had called the Dean on a whim - and here he was with another credential to add to his burgeoning résumé - a college Professor of Accounting.

Marcus was fun to be around. He told grand stories of worldly travels and of life and death escapades, including a stint as a mercenary in some Latin American country that he couldn't identify for security reasons, where he had suffered an injury to his leg, which caused his slight limp.

The students took to Marcus immediately. Partly this was because, in that rather staid and formal era, where all teachers were addressed as Mr. Jones, Dr. Smith, or Professor Anderson, Steven Marcus Becker insisted that they call him *Marcus*. It was the first time that any teacher at our little college had ever allowed students to call them by their first name, or in this case, had encouraged them to do so, and they loved it.

Another thing that the students loved about Marcus was that he informed them that the classroom would be run democratically. The students would decide how much homework was necessary in order for them to learn the material. The students would also decide when, or if, there would be exams and they would help set the grading scale. Obviously, having this amount of involvement in organizing the class and in determining grades for the course was a big hit with the students.

You might recall that I previously mentioned the ADVANCE program offered for Vietnam veterans as a night school program at our college. The veterans attended classes on Tuesday and Thursday nights, were considered full-time students, and thus received their full veteran's education payment, which far exceeded their cost of tuition and books for the courses. Many of the students made no bones about the fact that the easier a course was the better they liked it since they were only in it for the money.

I offered an Investments class that met on Thursday

night the first week of the semester and was greeted by over 70 students. Since most of our classrooms were set up to hold 35 or 40 students, we rolled back the movable room divider between two rooms to have enough space to accommodate my large group. This meant that I was in a room that was actually two rooms deep – about 70 or 80 feet deep. Not a very good situation for teaching a group of over 70 veterans from 9 p.m. to midnight.

The morning after that first Investments class, Marcus asked how the class had gone. I told him that it had the potential for disaster, with over 70 students and a double deep classroom. He said, "I know a little about investments, maybe they could divide the class in half and we'd each have a manageable class of about 35 students."

I was grateful for Marcus's offer and in return offered to provide him with all of my presentation notes and exams so he wouldn't have to prepare special materials for the class. The Dean approved dividing the class as we proposed. Marcus and I each set about teaching our Investments classes, using the same textbook and an identical set of presentation notes.

The first exam was scheduled for the fifth week of classes. I used the same exams for the ADVANCE classes that I used for my daytime classes, since they were, in fact, the same course, at least in theory. Marcus and I both gave the same exam to our respective classes.

The day after the first exam was administered, Marcus asked me how my students had done on the exam. I replied that the results were pretty normal for an ADVANCE class

– out of 100 possible points there were a couple of scores in the 90's, several in the 80's, a batch in the 70's and 60's, some in the 50's and 40's and a couple in the 30's. Marcus looked a little puzzled and then said smugly, "My lowest score was a 92."

Holy smoke. I had taught the course a dozen times to daytime college students and to several groups of ADVANCE students and never had results anywhere close to that – the results were always about like the results I had on this exam. Marcus was indeed a gifted teacher. Or, I was a dud. Or maybe it was some of each.

Marcus and I didn't discuss the exam any further, but during the week I contemplated what I might do in the future to bring my students results up to the level of Marcus's class. Frankly, I had always been a very conscientious teacher and had always tried my best to do a good job, so I didn't know what else I might be able to do.

I walked into my classroom of ADVANCE Investments students the following Thursday night and they jumped me. "Why can't we use our books for the test?" "Why can't we use our notes?" "Why can't we work together on the test?" "Why can't we ask *you* for help on the test?"

The mystery of Marcus's students' mastery of my exam was solved. Marcus had failed to inform me of those few little details as he gloated about his students' fabulous results.

The ADVANCE investments course continued on like that for the rest of the semester. I taught my class and gave my exams in the traditional way; Marcus taught his section in his way. His students loved him; mine tolerated me.

Marcus's democratic classroom approach and his handling of the ADVANCE investments course were just the first two of many unique, unusual, unorthodox, strange, weird, and just plain goofy teaching procedures and techniques employed by Steven Marcus Becker.

About the middle of the semester, things started to unravel for Marcus. As it turned out, the serious, conscientious students who actually wanted to learn something or those who needed to maintain a certain grade point average to qualify for their scholarship did not want a course with little or no homework and a course where everybody got the same grade. They wanted a traditional course taught in the traditional way. By the end of the semester, even the students who originally thought Marcus was wonderful had turned on him for one reason or another.

When grades came out for the semester, Marcus's students found that he had basically graded by how well he liked someone personally, or by what they said or did not say about him on their course evaluations, rather than by their classroom performance. Some of the worst students got the best grades and some of the best students got the worst grades.

A horde of students marched on the Dean's office to complain about Marcus. The Dean was a chickenshit and said that he'd check into it, which he didn't, simply hoping that it would all go away. Go away it did not.

Marcus was given to grandiose plans, dreams, and schemes. And, once he got an idea, he prided himself on being a guy who would follow through and make it happen. One of his grand ideas was to have his accounting students provide a public service for the poor and elderly and to prepare their income tax returns for free.

Marcus called every newspaper in the area and they jumped on the idea, with some of them running front page stories about this wonderful service provided by the students of Marcus Becker. And, the articles stated, that even though the tax returns were going to be prepared by college accounting students, Professor Marcus Becker would review each return to make certain that it was accurate.

Marcus's income tax service resulted in two rather predictable occurrences. First, dozens of people, some of whom weren't so poor or so elderly, charged out to the college to take advantage of this wonderful free program. Second, every tax accountant and lawyer within five counties called the College to complain about how the College, which was taxpayer supported, was competing with private businesses and cutting into their livelihood. By now, however, it was too late to stop the program since it was well underway.

The free income tax service program had several flaws. First, the accounting students, under the tutelage of Steven Marcus Becker, knew very little about accounting and virtually nothing about income taxes. Second, as it was now becoming apparent, Steven Marcus Becker knew little about accounting and probably nothing about income taxes.

The last day to file one's personal income taxes is April 15, as you well know. Well, starting around April 1, the people

Memoirs of a Recovering Teacher

who had taken advantage of the free Marcus Becker income tax service and who had dumped off all of their financial records at Marcus's office started calling to inquire about when their taxes would be done. And they continued to call every day. Finally, when the countdown was near – April 12, April 13, April 14 – they called three or four times per day. Marcus assured them that there was nothing to worry about, that their return would be ready the morning of April 15, and that they could pick it up at his office and get it filed on time.

On the morning of April 15, Marcus called in sick. Absolute bedlam broke out at the College when people came out to pick up their tax returns and found that their financial information, tax returns, and the guy who was to prepare them, Marcus Becker, were all missing. The Dean frantically called Marcus's home but got no answer. He went over to Marcus's trailer and banged on the door but got no answer. The Dean tracked down the students who were supposed to be doing the tax returns, but they all said that they knew nothing about income taxes so Marcus had said he would personally prepare each of the returns. The Dean took the liberty of searching Marcus's office for the missing financial information and tax returns but found nothing.

The following day, Marcus showed up for work like nothing had happened. He attributed it all to a big misunderstanding and said that he had it all under control. According to him, he had filed for an extension for each of his free tax service clients and he said that he'd get the returns filed within a week. Apparently he did that, since the whole thing quieted down within a few days. I never heard if any of the tax returns got audited, but if they did, I'm sure it would have taken a team of high-powered auditors to unravel the financial tales woven by one Steven Marcus Becker.

It's not unusual for a new teacher to have a rough first semester, but usually they learn a lot from their mistakes and improve greatly the following semester. For Marcus, it went the opposite way; things got worse as time went along and the students were in near riot mode by the end of the second semester.

Fortunately for everyone involved, Marcus was a job hopper and he applied for a job at another college. He was granted an interview, which apparently went very well – recall that Marcus could be a real charmer. The Accounting Department Chairperson at the new college called our Dean to ask for a recommendation. The normal procedure in the education field has always been, and still is, if you really want to get rid of someone, give him or her a wonderful recommendation and pawn your problem off on the next guy. That's what our Dean did and Marcus got the job and we got rid of him. The Dean wasn't such a chickenshit after all.

Marcus loaded up all of his stuff in a U-Haul trailer and headed out for his new position as Professor of Accounting at some college in Illinois – a larger and more prestigious college than ours. That was the last time that I ever saw Steven Marcus Becker. But, the story does not end here. In fact, the real story just begins.

About five years after Marcus left us for bigger and better

things in Illinois, I received a phone call from a newspaper reporter from the *Quad-City Times*, which serves the Quad Cities of Rock Island and Moline, Illinois and Bettendorf and Davenport, Iowa. He said that he was writing a newspaper story on a guy named Steven Marcus Becker and wondered if he could interview me. I was happy to oblige. I had wondered from time to time what had happened to Marcus and I figured that this reporter was about to satisfy my curiosity. Nothing would have surprised me, but I assumed that Marcus was now president of some college or something like that – he was a charmer, you know, and he did have grandiose plans, dreams, and schemes. I was about to be shocked.

The reporter explained that the person that I knew as Steven Marcus Becker was, in fact, an imposter. He had assumed the identity of the real Steven Marcus Becker some seven or eight years ago and had been passing himself off as such ever since. He didn't know who Marcus really was, where he came from, or why he had assumed the other man's identity, but he did know a lot about his activities after he left our college.

Marcus had apparently learned enough about accounting and teaching while at our college to impress them mightily at his new college in Illinois. Towards the end of Marcus's first year there, the department chairperson resigned and they appointed Marcus the Accounting Department Chairman. He had once again moved into a position that he knew nothing about (This is called the *Peter Principle*, which, by the way, was not named by or after me) and it ended up disastrously, just as his teaching position at our college had. He got into a fistfight with one of the instructors in his department and had threatened to murder another of them. The office secretary was so afraid of him that she often hid beneath her desk.

Apparently sensing that things were not going well in his new position, Marcus applied for an accounting teaching position at a university in Wisconsin. The University eagerly grabbed the opportunity to hire an Accounting Department Chairman to teach for them and hired him on the spot, after, of course, a glowing recommendation from his former employer in Illinois.

Marcus apparently adopted a low profile at the university in Wisconsin and taught there for two years without drawing attention to himself. Until, that is, when he taught a night class for senior citizens and swindled a couple of them out of over fifty thousand dollars on some grand scheme of his. The senior citizens finally figured out that Marcus had swindled them and went to the authorities.

A detective interviewed Marcus and Marcus was congenial, cooperative, and mystified. Apparently, there was some misunderstanding, he explained and suggested that he and the two senior citizens should meet with the detective the following day to try to sort it out. The detective agreed.

Within two hours, Marcus loaded up a U-Haul trailer and disappeared, not to be heard from since.

The reporter had interviewed everyone that he could find who had come in contact with "Dr. X," as he was calling Marcus, and was about to print his story exposing Dr. X to the world. I was able to provide very little information that the reporter did not already know, but he very much enjoyed Marcus's free income tax service story. "Vintage Dr. X," he had called it.

About three days after the reporter called, an FBI agent showed up at my house to interview me about Marcus. We lived in a small development on the edge of town and I was a real neighborhood hero for a few days for having a bona fide "G Man" come to see me.

Whereas the *Quad-City Times* reporter was willing to tell me everything that he knew about Marcus, the FBI guy refused to tell me anything – he was there to gather information, not to give it. He did say, though, that they had been on his trail for around seven years, which led me to believe that he must have done something pretty big – or should we say *grandiose*, to attract the attention of the FBI for that number of years.

After the FBI agent left my house, I thought back to all of the stories that Marcus had enthralled us with, particularly in the first few weeks he was at our college, before we started to get onto him and came to believe that most of his knowledge and stories were coming straight from the *National Enquirer*. I wondered if Marcus had actually bragged to us about the criminal activity that got him into trouble with the FBI and we didn't even know it.

There was one story, for instance, that he told about moving to a town in Ohio or Indiana or somewhere around there. He noticed immediately that there was a drastic shortage of college student housing. In a matter of four months he purchased around fifteen rental houses and small apartment buildings without putting in a penny of his own money. He said that he bought only properties that had been on the market for a long time and where the owners were desperate to sell. He bought them on contract from the owner and promised to give them a down payment within three months of when he took possession of the house. Then, he rented out the property and took the tenant's rental deposits and used them to pay the seller the down payment. Using the tenant's rental deposits for down payments to buy other properties is undoubtedly not legal, but I wonder if it was illegal enough to get the FBI involved.

Marcus told another story that was so far-fetched that I dismissed it as being another one of his tall tales. But, if true, I think it's the type of thing that might get the FBI on your trail, forever.

According to Marcus, he had owned a mobile home park in Louisiana. He dealt in brand new and used mobile homes and rented them out or sold them to buyers who lived in them and paid him a monthly lot rent. Somewhere along the line, he devised a scheme where he would take the title to each of the mobile homes to numerous banks and borrow money from each of them, pledging the same mobile home to each bank as security. When the banks finally got onto him and came to investigate, Marcus said that he took off all of the tongues, which contain the mobile home's serial number, and switched them around to different mobile homes. Then, he took all of the appliances, which also have serial numbers, and switched them around to different mobile homes. And he continued to switch all sorts of stuff around to different mobile homes than where they belonged.

When the lenders came to check on the mobile homes that were pledged as security for their loans, it was such a scrambled mess that they couldn't identify anything. Marcus had ended his story at that point with a hearty laugh.

I suspect, however, that the story might have continued on something like this: The lenders go to the police, who go to Marcus's trailer park to investigate. It is such a scrambled mess that they can't figure it out, but Marcus, the charmer, promises to assemble all of the records and to meet with them the next day. Within hours of their visit, Marcus loads up a U-Haul trailer and disappears. The local police, recognizing that they have been duped and realizing that Marcus somehow must have committed one or more federal crimes, call in the FBI.

In the meantime, Marcus somehow stumbles across the real Steven Marcus Becker and strikes up an engaging conversation with him. He learns where the real Steven Marcus Becker went to college, what he majored in, and so on, and probably swipes his billfold with his social security number and driver's license. With a little imagination and a little luck, there are now two Steven Marcus Beckers – one of whom prefers to be called *Marcus*. Another mystery solved.

How did our Marcus get away with stealing someone else's identity for so long, you might ask. Well, this was back in the mid 1970's – before computers and all of the electronic capabilities of today that can be used to double check tax records, social security numbers, and suspicious activities. It was in an era when you might hear about someone stealing someone else's identity or being an imposter maybe once in a decade – it was simply unheard of in those days. He probably would have gotten away with it forever, or at least until technology was created that could catch someone like him, if he hadn't fallen back into his old habits and scammed those senior citizens.

As clever as Marcus was, he blew his once-in-a-lifetime chance to make the big score – the type of score that every criminal mind lies awake nights dreaming about, and he didn't even know it. You see Marcus was at our college when personal computers were in their infancy. Our college had decided to start a Computer Specialist Program the following year and Marcus had convinced the Dean that he knew enough about computers to be the instructor in the program.

Our college owned a large mainframe computer and served as a regional Computer Center for over fifty public school systems in our section of the state. The Computer Center prepared class schedules and grade reports, and did the payroll for all of those schools. The Computer Specialist Program that Marcus was going to head up was to be housed in the room adjoining the Computer Center and Marcus would have been in and out of the Computer Center a dozen times a day.

As Marcus became a little bit familiar with the Computer Center, he would have discovered what I observed when I was in and out of the Computer Center every now and then to visit a friend who worked there. That is, in the wooden cabinet along the south wall were boxes and boxes of blank checks for each of the fifty plus school districts that the Computer Center processed payroll for – thousands of blank checks, to make it clear. That is, in a wooden cabinet that didn't even have a lock on it. In the wooden cabinet that Marcus would have discovered in his first day or two as the Computer Specialist Program teacher.

Marcus would have had a key to the Computer Center so he could come and go at any hour of the day or night. And, it would have been a simple matter to take a few dozen blank checks out of the bottom of each box, that no one would miss for months. From there he could have easily set up a shell company and written hundreds of checks on these school district checks to his shell company totaling millions of dollars. Then he could have wired the money to an off shore account and could have disappeared to some foreign country and lived a life of luxury forever.

You know Marcus well enough by now to know that he would have been unable to resist the challenge of doing exactly what I described here, and he would have done it. He would have had no choice but to do it. So, Marcus, ol' buddy, you blew it – you missed the big kill.

About five years after my call from the *Quad-City Times* reporter and my visit from the FBI, an administrator at our college told me that he had been informed that the FBI had finally caught our Marcus. He had no other details, except that he was sentenced to hard time in the big house, so I can't even speculate on how, when, or where they got him. Nor can I speculate on where he might be today. Wherever he is and whatever he's doing, however, I'm sure he is mesmerizing his listeners with grand tales of worldly travels and life and death escapades – and of his successful career as a college Accounting professor.

"Bridges"

The Bridges of Madison County was one of the biggest selling hardcover novels of all time and was made into a blockbuster movie. The movie came to our community soon after it was released.

One day I ran into the Psychology teacher in the hallway and he asked me, "Have you seen *The Bridges of Madison County* since it came to town?"

"No," I replied, "but my wife and I are planning on going tonight."

"Observe," he said.

"What am I looking for?" I asked.

"You'll know," he said.

Oh, those psychology types.

I ran into the Psychology teacher in the hallway the following day.

"Did you see *The Bridges of Madison County*? He asked.

"Yes," I replied.

"Well?" he asked.

"My wife and I were the youngest ones in the audience

– was that it?"

"That was it," he said, and he turned and walked away.

Oh, those psychology types.

"Lil Hitchhiker"

Lakes Community College had campuses in two communities about twenty-five miles apart, 'Ville and 'Burg. Occasionally, there was not a large enough demand for a particular course taught at the 'Burg campus to justify a full-time instructor on that campus, so an instructor from the 'Ville campus would commute to the 'Burg campus to teach that course. The commuting instructors would make the trip two or three times per week, depending on the course schedule. They were paid mileage for the fifty-mile round trip.

An instructor who commuted three days a week would rack up about 2,250 miles in a fifteen-week semester. At thirty-five cents a mile, they would receive $787.50 for mileage, which would cover the cost of their gas and maybe wear and tear on their vehicle.

Occasionally, some of the faculty were quite ingenious. One guy, who happened to be the same guy who had the car drive over him during halftime of a football game, found a way to make a profit off of the mileage. There was a slow-moving train that ran from 'Ville to 'Burg on a daily basis. He had their schedule down pat and would stow away on the train for his ride to 'Burg. He would teach his class and hitchhike back to 'Ville. At the end of the semester, he turned in mileage and collected $787.50 – pure profit. Ingenious, no?

Television Stars

Lakes Community College had two main campuses and three outlying centers where students could also take a limited number of courses. Faculty often had to commute 50-100 miles, round trip, to the outlying centers to teach a class or two, which resulted in the College paying a significant amount of money for the commuters' mileage.

The College made an application for a federal grant to receive money to install a television system whereby courses could be taught on TV at the two main campuses and broadcast to the other campus and outlying centers. The grant was approved and the television system was installed.

There were two television studio classrooms on each of the two main campuses, from which courses were broadcast. Students who enrolled for the course at the site from which it was broadcast were in the classroom with the instructor "live." The only difference from a traditional "live" class was that the course was also being transmitted to the other campus and centers via television. Students who took the course at the other campus or outlying centers watched the instructor on a television set.

The instructor had a battery-operated microphone that clipped onto their shirt or coat, exactly like those used by personalities on network television. The instructor's microphone was portable and had great range, so the instructor could move all over the classroom and be heard perfectly. The microphone had an on/off switch and when it was "on" the microphone was live all of the time. If a teacher didn't want to be heard over the television system, they had to remember to turn off their microphone. For instance, if a teacher was called out into the hallway by a secretary or an administrator for a message, the students could hear every word if the microphone wasn't turned off.

There was one occurrence, for instance, where a teacher finished teaching her television course and forgot to remove her microphone. Students in the following television class could hear every sound as she exited the building, opened her car door, closed the car door, turned on the engine, revved it up, and shifted into gear. They lost sound when she got to the intersection.

There was another occurrence in the early days of classroom television where the instructor kept his microphone on while the students labored over an examination. The students in his broadcast classroom all seemed trustworthy and there were adults monitoring the exam in the outlying television classrooms, so he decided to slip out for a little break. The students could hear every sound as he walked down the hallway, said "Hello" to a couple of colleagues, hummed a little tune to himself, and opened the door - to the men's restroom. You can use your imagination from there.

The Booksellers

If you have purchased college textbooks in recent years you know that they are very costly, often running $75 - $150 each.

There are several reasons why textbooks are so costly,

including that they are usually very large books and that they are often hard cover books, which cost about twice as much as paperbacks to produce. There's another reason that college textbooks are so expensive that is not well known by the general public and that you may find interesting.

Let's say that the history teacher decides to choose a new textbook to teach from for the upcoming school year. Let's also assume that there are ten different textbook publishers that publish history textbooks and that each publisher has two different titles available. So, there are twenty different textbooks available on the market for the teacher to choose from.

All the teacher has to do is contact each of the publishers and request a complimentary review copy of each title and the publishers will gladly send out free copies of the textbooks for the teacher to review. If the teacher adopts their text, it may result in the publisher selling hundreds of copies of the textbook to that college per year for many years.

The teacher studies each of the complimentary textbooks that they received, makes a selection of the text to use for their classes, and informs the bookstore to order the books for the students to buy for the course. The teacher places the other nineteen review copies on the bookshelves in their office to use for future reference purposes, and to serve as professorial office decoration.

Here's where the good part comes in. Sometime during the school year, a person known as a *used book buyer* stops in to visit the teacher and notices the nineteen brand new textbooks on the bookshelves. The used book buyer offers the teacher cash, say $400, for those nineteen books. The teacher accepts, the used book buyer forks over four $100 bills, and carts away the nineteen textbooks. The used book buyer then hauls the books back to his company's warehouse and his company sells the books to other colleges at a discount – cheaper than the book's publisher would sell them to that college.

So, to summarize, the textbook publisher withstood the cost of writing, editing, printing, binding, and marketing the books and gave them to the teacher for free as review copies. The teacher sold them to the used book buyer's company, who sells them to colleges, in competition with the publisher who created the books in the first place. And, the author who wrote the book and the publisher who published it receive no money at all for those books – zero. Therefore, to cover these huge losses, the publisher has to raise the price of the textbooks that it publishes.

Most college teachers only order review copies when they are actually planning to adopt a new textbook and they do, in fact, adopt one of the books that they received as review copies. Also, many college teachers believe it is unethical to sell their review copies to the used book buyers, so they keep them on their shelves for reference purposes or even send them back to the publishers.

There are always a few people who take advantage of the situation and I knew several teachers who, in essence, operated a used book business, ordering review copies of textbooks for courses where they had no intention of making a new adoption.

One fellow, Harlan, was particularly blatant. The only subject that he taught was History, but he ordered review copies for every discipline taught at the College including English, Marketing, Sales, Accounting, Economics, Math, Geography, Speech, Psychology, Spanish, Sociology, Chemistry, Biology – you name it and he ordered review copies for it. He had a sophisticated ordering system and proudly bragged that he had once received ninety-five books in a single week.

There are numerous college textbook publishers, but only a few have sales representatives that call upon the teachers personally. Most of the publishers simply publish catalogs and flyers that they mail to the teachers. That is one of the reasons why Harlan was able to operate his used book business so successfully. That is, until one day a representative from one of the publishers showed up unexpectedly on campus with a computer printout about six feet long listing complimentary review copies they had sent out. He walked into the faculty lounge and said, "I'm looking for a guy named Harlan." And you could tell by the tone of his voice that it wasn't a social call.

Word got to Harlan through the grapevine that this guy was looking for him and Harlan hid out in the furnace room the rest of the afternoon. Harlan's business collapsed after that close call.

There are numerous used book buyers and the competition among them is fierce. It was particularly interesting when two competing book buyers showed up on campus on the same day. It sometimes resulted in a confrontation and one time, a used book buyer chased another off campus by threatening to kill him if he didn't leave.

Signs

My office at Lakes Community College had a large window about three feet high and four feet wide, allowing me to observe the adjoining classroom. When the building was built, the classroom was used to teach Secretarial Machines, Office Machines, and Calculating Machines and the window was installed so I could keep an eye on the valuable equipment in the classroom. Through the years as technology changed, much of the equipment was removed and the classroom was used primarily for traditional lecture courses. The window remained, however. There was a drape on the window so I could cover the window or leave it open, as I chose.

The classroom was set up with tables and chairs facing the front, which was the far wall from my office. Thus, students would sit with their backs to my window and the instructor would be at the front of the room facing the students, and facing my window.

I had a lot of fun through the years peering out of that window at my colleagues as they blazed away imparting truth, wisdom, and knowledge to an unsuspecting and, often, uninterested assemblage. My most fun, though, was when I would craft a sign with large letters saying something like "Your zipper is down," or "Bullshit," or "You gotta be kidding," and hold it up for the teacher to see.

Without fail, my sign would startle the teacher, cause them to lose concentration, make them blush, or make them laugh. The students would instantly whip around to look at the window in the back of the room to see what was going on and, of course, by then I had ducked out of the way, leaving them to wonder, "What in the hell was that all about?"

Occasionally, when I was in that same classroom imparting said truth, wisdom, and knowledge, one of my colleagues would sneak into my office and pay me back.

Besides adding depth to my little office, that window gave me a view of education in action that few people ever get a chance to observe, and it gave me some of my fondest memories as a teacher.

If anyone reading this was a student in one of those classes in that room when your instructor suddenly broke out laughing or started to blush for no apparent reason, you now know the rest of the story. And you also now know that even though we on the faculty took our job seriously, we weren't serious all of the time.

The Poison Pen

As a teacher, the one thing that you can always count on is that, in the eyes of the faculty, the administration will foul things up miserably at least two or three times a year and consequently they will become the subject of ridicule and the butt of jokes in the faculty lounge.

During the last twenty years or so that I taught at Lakes

Community College, almost every time that the administration made a colossal goof up, someone would write a tongue-in-cheek, satirical dissertation lampooning the administration for their ineptness. Sometimes, the writing appeared the day after the screw-up; sometimes it would take a week. You'd show up in the morning, go to the faculty lounge to get your mail, and there it was in your mailbox and the mailbox of every faculty member – *the memo*, written by the anonymous Poison Pen.

Each new memo was read carefully, as faculty members analyzed what it said, what it didn't say, and what it said between the lines. The memos were a lighthearted spoof and were obviously intended to be a humorous expose, taking a good-natured jab at the administration. They were never mean spirited and seemed to be intended for harmless fun. Nevertheless, the memos often contained hard-hitting truths.

There was a time, for instance, that the college President sent a memo to every faculty member, saying that the college was over budget and exhorting everyone to immediately initiate whatever cost cutting measures that they could in their use of school supplies. Since the memo came out two weeks before the start of the faculty's salary negotiations with the administration, the message was viewed skeptically as an initial bargaining ploy by the administration – "We're broke and can't give anybody a pay raise."

In view of the fact that the college had a fifty million dollar budget, the idea of the faculty being able to cut enough costs on school supplies to bail out the administration apparently seemed ludicrous to the holder of the poison pen. The memo that showed up in the faculty mailboxes is shown below. As with most things, you "had to be there" to get the full impact of the situation that caused the memo to be written in the first place and to fully appreciate the message as seen through the eyes of the faculty at that point in time. Nevertheless, you'll get the idea.

MEMO

TO: The Administration
FROM: I.M. Concerned
RE: Cost Cutting Measures

Thank you for asking for my ideas on how the college can avoid financial disaster. I believe that the following measures will result in significant savings and provide the college with a budget surplus within only two or three weeks:

1. When sending out memos like the one encouraging efficient use of supplies, do not send one to every person. Send only one announcement for posting on the bulletin board in the faculty lounge. If the memo contains anything worthwhile, word will get around.

2. Remove all chalk from classrooms and issue each teacher a glass of water. They can dip their finger in the water and write on the chalkboard with their wet finger. This has the side benefit of training students how to become fast note takers.

3. Move the night classes to the daytime, thus saving electricity.

4. Lease out the fleet of school cars on the weekends.

5. Install a wood burning furnace and burn student papers and exams for fuel.

6. Switch the natural gas furnace to a human gas furnace. An hour after lunch is consumed in the college cafeteria, there is enough human gas on campus to power the furnace for a week.

7. Save money by eliminating repair and maintenance of equipment and vehicles; let the next President worry about it.

8. Sell beer in the student center. The college will make a fortune and it will liven up classes.

9. Switch to a four-day academic week, Monday through Thursday. All classes will meet on a Monday-Wednesday or Tuesday-Thursday schedule for an hour and a half each day. Lock the building down for a three-day weekend and turn off everything including the heat and the lights.

10. Reducing the academic week by twenty percent, from five days to four days, should likewise result in a twenty percent reduction in administrators – fire one-fifth of them, now.

Thank you for asking for my help, advice, assistance, and recommendations. If I can help in any other way, please let me know. P.S. A statement for my consulting fee of $500 is attached.

Some of the faculty boasted of having a complete set of the Poison Pen memos and if a faculty member's mailbox was skipped when a new memo came out, they felt slighted.

There was as much speculation and discussion about who wrote the memos and how they got them into the mailboxes in the faculty lounge without being spotted, as there was about the content of the memos themselves. Since the memos always had the same format and writing style, it was widely believed that the memos were being written by the same person, or persons, every time. Was it Armstrong who writes the memos? How about Sanders? Maybe it's Schendel or Berven or Wilson or Larson. Perhaps it's Jones – no, not Jones. But, it could be Grems or Purdy or Harms or Hubers or Walz.

No one stepped forth to take the credit, or the blame, for writing the memos, although from time to time when a particularly clever memo surfaced, there was a person or two that didn't deny it when their name came up. They seemed to like the image of being considered worthy to have written the memo.

The administration was most likely unaware of most of the memos, as they were distributed only to the faculty via the faculty mailboxes. Oh, occasionally one of the memos must have made its way into the hands of an administrator, because they would make some comment at a meeting like, "Somebody seems to have a lot of time on their hands," in obvious reference to a recent memo.

The administration probably chose the correct strategy in ignoring the memos and not trying to find the perpetrator. Starting an investigation would have been an invitation for open warfare with not only the Poison Pen, but also with a dozen Poison Pen wannabes who would have jumped into the foray and peppered the administration with a blizzard of memos.

Through the years, some of those suspected of being the Poison Pen retired or moved on to other jobs, but the memos kept on coming – it hadn't been them after all.

There were a few people who knew who the Poison Pen

was, but they did not divulge the identity, at least not until the Poison Pen had left the College for other ventures.

How did the Poison Pen get the memos into the mailboxes without being detected? Simply, the Poison Pen worked later at the College each day than just about everybody on the faculty, except for the computer CAD teacher who basically lived there, and put the memos in the mailboxes before going home. It was widely assumed that the memos were placed in the mailboxes in the morning by some early riser, which helped the Poison Pen maintain their cover.

Many on the faculty had fun reading the memos, dissecting them, discussing them, and occasionally, laughing at them. Undoubtedly none of them had as much fun as the Poison Pen, though, writing them and then waiting to see what response the latest memo would receive.

One fall semester, the administration pulled a couple of classic boo-boos. Uncharacteristically, and sadly, no Poison Pen memos arrived in the faculty mailboxes. People analyzed who had retired the previous spring, put two and two together, and were finally able to identify the Poison Pen. This was verified by some of the faculty who had been in the know all along.

A friend at the college told me about one of the greatest compliments that I have ever received. About a year after I retired from the college, someone took a stab at crafting a Poison Pen memo. It was read and discussed in the faculty lounge and someone speculated that, "Maybe Peterson is back."

Someone in the room replied curtly, "It's not good enough to be a Peterson." What a wonderful thing to have said about one's work.

Faculty Meetings

It seems that some school administrators' idea of working is to call a meeting. I'll admit that some meetings are necessary to foster a discussion or to distribute information. The ones that bugged me were the regularly-scheduled meetings that were held every week or every month whether there was anything of value to discuss or not. It was time to meet so, dammit, we met.

The meetings were usually pretty boring, but occasionally there would be a comment from the audience that livened things up. There was one faculty member, for instance, who would address some administrator's harebrained proposition with a comment such as, "That sounds just like the story about the donkey and the goat," and then he would laugh like a crazed madman. None of us knew what the hell he was talking about, but it was so goofy that we couldn't help but laugh, too.

This chorus of laughter from the faculty apparently suckered the administrator into thinking that we all knew the story about the donkey and the goat and how it applied to this situation. They didn't want to look like a dummy and ask for an explanation of the donkey and goat story, so often they backed off of their harebrained idea. Maybe that's what the guy had in mind.

Elvis Was Here

Attendance at faculty meetings called by the administration was mandatory. An attendance sheet was passed around for everyone to sign. It may not have occurred to the administration, but with over a hundred people in attendance, it would have been easy for someone to sign in a buddy who wasn't there – not that this ever occurred, mind you.

For at least my last ten years on the job, someone would sign the attendance sheet by printing the name, ELVIS, in bold red letters. It became a tradition and many of the faculty looked forward to seeing if ELVIS had signed in when the attendance sheet came around. It didn't take much to amuse us at a faculty meeting.

The office secretaries who kept track of faculty meeting attendance often speculated about who was signing in as ELVIS. A couple of them analyzed the handwriting and came to the conclusion that the name was always written by the same person. Even the Dean got in on the act in trying to figure out who was ELVIS. It was harmless fun, but it was one of those little mysteries that everyone would like to know the answer to. Obviously, some of the faculty, who saw ELVIS sign in, knew who it was, but they were not about to give up the *King*.

And In This Corner, Weighing In At…

To amuse myself, and hopefully some of my colleagues at one of the faculty meetings, I wrote the following memo and passed it around for a few of them to read.

TO WHOM IT MAY CONCERN

Following is a partial list of people in this room that I think I can whip:
1. Dean Smith
2. Alyssa
3. Marion the Librarian
4. George
5. Assistant Dean, Betty
6. Martha
7. Theodore
8. Carol
9. Dennis (The psychology teacher, not the coach)
10. Delores

Signed: Dave Peterson

George took offense and said that he didn't think I could take him. To settle the matter, I crossed his name off the list.

Faculty Lounge Under Attack

Some of the more interesting faculty meetings were the *Faculty Association* meetings. The Faculty Association was made up entirely of faculty members and the purpose of the Association was to further matters of interest, concern, or importance to the faculty. For instance, if the administration proposed something that the faculty didn't like, the Faculty Association would send a memo to the administration or request a meeting. There was strength in numbers and banding together often achieved a better result than an individual would have been able to obtain by him or herself.

The one factor, however, that often rendered the Faculty Association to be far less effective and less powerful than it could have been is that when a controversy arose, the first thing we usually did was to choose up sides and fight each other. By the time that we got done fighting each other, we didn't have enough fight left in us to battle the real enemy.

I recall one time, though, when everyone in the Faculty Association was in total agreement. Looking back at it, we should have seen it coming when a year before the administration started calling the faculty lounge the *faculty workroom*. And now, the administration announced that they were going to take the faculty workroom and turn it into office space.

In the eyes of the faculty, the faculty lounge is the most sacred room in the entire building, if not in the whole town, or maybe the entire state. It was a safe haven for faculty where no student dared to enter. It was a place to relax and unwind on one of the mismatched, but revered, chairs or couches. It was the place where great stories about students were shared and where gossip about the administration was enjoyed. It was hallowed ground and, dammit, there would be a fight before it was surrendered.

A stinging memo was sent from the Faculty Association to the administration, demanding a face-to-face meeting to discuss the matter of closing the faculty lounge. Whether the memo should call the room the *faculty lounge* or the *faculty workroom* was hotly debated and it was finally decided that we would stand up to the administration and call it what it rightfully was, the *faculty lounge*.

The administration had apparently misjudged the faculty's reverence for the faculty lounge and the faculty's resolve, so they simply let the matter die. The faculty lounge remained a sacred haven for the faculty as it always had been and was always meant to be.

I was told that about three years after I retired, the administration successfully closed the faculty lounge and turned it into office space. I am glad that I was not there to witness this sad end to a time-honored tradition.

After having been a teacher for all those years, though, I know this – the administration may have been able to take the lounge from the faculty, but there is no way that they were able to take the faculty from the lounge. Somewhere in the bowels of the building - maybe in the back of the furnace room or in some storeroom – there is a group of faculty sitting on mismatched furniture telling stories about students and gossiping about the administration.

The Great Debate

Just about every teacher that I have ever known felt that they carried the heaviest load, worked the hardest, or had the most difficult job on the faculty.

The English teachers may have had only two or three preparations but they had mountains of student essays to read and correct, all of which were written by amateurs who thought that their work was equal to Shakespeare at his best.

The computer teachers had to constantly keep up with

new software and technology and needed to keep one step ahead of the hackers in their classes. The social science teachers had to continually be aware of social issues in the world and how they affected the present and future. The math teachers' subject matter may not have changed for decades, but they had to keep abreast of the newest theories of how to teach mathematics and had to try to untangle student calculations so they could point out where they had gone wrong.

The science teachers had to comply with ever-increasing environmental issues and had to conduct numerous laboratory experiments and create laboratory assignments for students, all without blowing up the place. The Psychology teachers had to deal with some of the most dangerous people on earth – students who had taken one or two psychology courses and thought that they were the second coming of Sigmund Freud.

The speech teachers may have had only one or two preparations and were articulate enough to teach the course without even opening a textbook, but they had to suffer through listening to hours of boring speeches by tongue-tied amateurs suffering from stage fright. And we business teachers often had four or five different courses to teach per semester, which required a huge amount of preparation in addition to keeping abreast of what was happening in the business world.

Even though each of us thought that ours was the toughest discipline to teach, and that most of the rest of the faculty had a softer job than us for one reason or the other, I doubt that any of us would have switched jobs with anyone else.

That Leisurely Lifestyle

You might recall that one of my reasons for choosing teaching as a career was that I perceived it to be a leisurely occupation where teachers worked from maybe 8:00 a.m. to 3:30 p.m. When I got my first teaching position in high school, I found that I was horribly mistaken.

When I had been a student in college, it was possible to have a flirting acquaintance with the subject matter and to still get by – maybe you'd get a "B" or a "C" for a grade, but you could get by. I soon discovered that as the teacher, when I was going to present a particular topic, I had to know *everything* about that topic. Even though I got good grades as a college student, I did not actually learn the subject matter in any of my business courses until I started to teach them, I mean *really* learn it. That required me to spend many hours a day, and night, and weekends, studying the textbooks that I was teaching from and doing additional research to master the material and to devise techniques and methods to explain it to students so they could comprehend it. Not exactly a five-day-a-week, 8:00 to 3:30 job.

The number of days in a teacher's contract at Lakes Community College varied from 180 days to 220 days, depending upon the type of program or courses that a person taught. For my 34-year career at the College, my annual contract was usually for ten and a half months, resulting in 200 work days per year. During those thirty-four years, I normally skipped lunch, except for maybe twenty times per year, choosing to, or needing to, work in my office instead.

Therefore, by usually skipping lunch, I worked an extra 180 hours a year for 34 years, or a total of 6,120 extra hours. This means, based on a 200-day year and 8-hour workday, that I worked an extra 3.83 years in my 34-year career at Lakes Community College. What an idiot I was.

Some leisurely lifestyle, huh?

Administrators

I previously mentioned the quotation about teachers that is attributed to George Bernard Shaw, *"Those who can, do. Those who can't, teach."* I refuted that clever saying as being largely untrue.

Someone added on another line to that saying, *"Those who can't teach, teach teachers."* That is also cute and clever, and I suspect whoever came up with that was thinking of faculty in-service presenters. When considered in that light, the saying appears to have more than a little merit.

Someone added yet another line to the saying, *"Those who can't teach teachers, become school administrators."* I suspect that many teachers would agree that this saying also has some merit.

From my experience as a teacher, I'd estimate that about three-fourths of the administrators that I worked with were solid educators, competent, good leaders, good communicators, and good people who treated the faculty and staff with respect. The other one fourth were, well, good fodder for the stories that I am about to relate to you.

"Listen, People"

Our accounting teacher resigned in April, effective at the end of June, so we had ample time to find a replacement before the start of fall classes. The position was advertised widely and we had over twenty well-qualified applicants. We selected three of them to come to campus for personal interviews. Any of the three would have been acceptable for the job but we could only hire one. We unanimously decided to offer the job to Beverly, who was a woman in her late twenties with a Master's Degree in accounting, CPA certification, public accounting experience, and several years of teaching experience. And, she had personality plus.

In those days, the Dean of Instruction was a man about fifty years old who was smart and who was a good educator with outstanding educational vision for the College. He was a handsome man who was a sharp dresser and who could be very articulate and charming. However, on occasion, he also had a mean streak.

Normally, when the Dean conducted a meeting, he would do an admirable job of explaining the information that he had in mind and of describing what the group was to do. If someone raised a legitimate question, he would answer it without getting irritated, usually. But, if someone raised what he perceived to be an *objection* to what he was proposing, the Dean would instantly become combative and would give us his famous Listen, People speech. It went something like this: "Listen people – if you're going to be negative, if you're not going to be supportive and get behind what we're trying to do here, if all you're going to do is complain, then you can just get out and go on down the road. Get out – now. We don't need you. We don't want you. We can get along without you. Just get out – now. Go. Get out."

It was one of the funniest damn things I ever heard. I heard the *Listen, People* speech several times a year and actually looked forward to it, just as long as it wasn't aimed specifically at me.

Our new accounting teacher, Beverly, showed up for work early her first day on the job. She had a big smile on her face, was enthusiastic, excited, and eager to get started.

Beverly left our Business Department office a few minutes before 9 a.m. saying she was going to the cafeteria for the *New Employee's Breakfast.*

About an hour later, Beverly came staggering through the door of our office; her face was as white as a sheet of typing paper.

"How was the New Employee's Breakfast? I asked.

"That man – the Dean," she said. "He started out by saying how happy he was that we were all here and told us that he'd do anything that he could to help make our tenure here pleasant and productive – and then he got this mean look on his face and said, but *Listen, People…*"

Beverly must have thought that her new colleagues in the Business Department were a bunch of heartless lunatics when we all simultaneously broke out in laughter – rolling on the floor laughter. After the laughter subsided, we explained to her that she had simply been introduced to the Dean's Listen, People speech and that she could expect to hear it two or three times a year.

Beverly became one of the most valued professors at Lakes Community College with a career that spanned some thirty years. And, she was there long after the Dean decided that he should *Get out and go on down the road.*

The Book Club

Two faculty members, Judy and Barb, were having lunch in the college cafeteria when the Assistant Dean joined them. They chitchatted about the weather, movies, and students until the Assistant Dean steered the discussion to books. She said that she was reading a fabulous book titled *The Psychology of Motivation* and that she was sure both Judy and Barb would enjoy the book also. In fact, she was so sure that they would enjoy it that she volunteered to give each of them a copy of the book. And then she had another idea – what fun it would be for each of them to read, say, two chapters a week and to get together every Friday to discuss the two chapters that they had read. This was the Assistant Dean, and Judy and Barb felt they had no choice but to agree to become part of *The Book Club*.

The Assistant Dean provided each of them with a copy of the book that same afternoon and reminded them that they should read the first two chapters and be prepared to discuss them at The Book Club the next Friday.

Judy and Barb dutifully read the first two chapters of *The Psychology of Motivation* and met the Assistant Dean as scheduled on Friday afternoon to discuss the material.

The Assistant Dean led the discussion, "Are new college graduates seeking their first job more motivated by money or by the challenge of the job?" "What is the driving force that compels some people to want to excel at a high level?" "Why do you think that some people are afraid of success?" "What are the three universal things that motivate most people?" "Are people more motivated by fear or by reward?"

The Assistant Dean did all of the asking of questions and Judy and Barb did all of the answering. The Assistant Dean did not offer any of her own views on the book.

The next week, the three of them met again and followed the same formula – the Assistant Dean asked the two of them a dozen questions about the book and Judy and Barb answered the questions.

After the third week, Judy and Barb were starting to get suspicious about what was going on, after the fourth week they were positive, and after the fifth week they didn't know if they should laugh or cry. But they were in too deep to do anything about it, and it was, after all the Assistant Dean.

What was going on, apparently, was that the Assistant Dean was enrolled in a college course where the assignment was to read the book *The Psychology of Motivation*. Each week she was to answer a set of questions about two chapters of the book. Instead of reading the book herself, however, she hoodwinked Judy and Barb into reading it under the ploy of being part of "The Book Club." Then, each Friday when they met, the Assistant Dean asked the two of them the questions that she was to answer for her homework assignment. After The Book Club session, the Assistant Dean undoubtedly ran back to her office and wrote down the answers that Judy and Barb had provided her with.

Judy and Barb considered sabotaging the Assistant Dean's weekly assignment by both calling in sick on a Friday, or by giving her bogus answers to her questions so she would flunk the course. But, when you're a member of a Book Club, that's no way to act, especially if the leader of The Book Club is the Assistant Dean – the same Assistant Dean who performs your annual teacher evaluation.

Besides, Judy and Barb really did enjoy reading *The Psychology of Motivation*. It was too bad that the Assistant Dean didn't have the pleasure of reading it.

Voter Strategy

Lakes Community College received revenue from several sources including student tuition and fees, state aid, and a local tax levy. The local tax levy was a tax paid by property owners in the geographic area served by the college and it came up for a vote for renewal every ten years. If renewed, the local tax levy would amount to millions of dollars over the ten-year period that would be used to maintain the buildings and to buy equipment. It was a very important source of revenue for the college. In fact, it would be difficult for the college to exist without it unless there were major budget cuts elsewhere.

State law said that the college could place the vote for the local tax levy on the ballot three years before the present tax levy expired. If it was voted down, the college could try again the next year and again the year after that, if necessary.

Since the college provided a wide range of services for residents of the area of all ages, the local tax levy vote had sailed through on the first try for over thirty years.

The strategy chosen by the administration to get the local tax levy vote passed this time was brilliant. They simply put it on the ballot and did not spend one minute or one dime on a marketing campaign to inform voters about what the tax levy money would be used for, that it amounted to an annual tax of only about five dollars on an average-priced home, or that it actually wasn't a new tax but was, instead, a renewal of an existing tax. Like I said, brilliant.

Two days before the scheduled vote, the area *Taxpayers Association,* a watchdog group that was against raising taxes, ran full-page ads in all of the area newspapers and ran radio ads throughout the area. Their message was simple – "The College is asking us to vote for a tax that they have not explained to us. Since more information is needed before we can make an intelligent decision about voting on this tax, we urge you to vote NO until more information can be obtained."

The Taxpayer's Association strategy worked beautifully. It planted doubt in voters' minds, and simply asked voters to postpone approving the levy until more information was available. Also, the Taxpayer's Association's timing was impeccable and the College did not have time to counteract the Association's message. The tax levy was voted down by a huge margin.

A few days after the devastating tax levy vote, a colleague in the Business Department and I were discussing what the college should have done to mount a successful campaign to inform voters about the local tax levy and to get the vote passed. We decided to take it one step further and in a half hour, we mapped out a strategy listing about twenty-five specific marketing ideas that would lead to getting the vote passed.

We asked the college President if he would like to see our marketing proposal and he was eager to meet with us. The College adopted our proposal and instituted it the next time the local tax levy vote came up and it passed by one of the widest margins ever.

As you have been reading my memoirs, I am sure you discovered that I was responsible for creating a small amount of chaos from time to time (keep reading, there's more). I believe that my helping to develop a marketing strategy to pass the local tax levy wiped the slate clean.

The Petition

Our college President and the Superintendent of a large school district in the area started taking potshots at each other, placing blame for all sorts of things and throwing dirt back and forth. The controversy had spilled over into the news media and it was making headlines on a daily basis. Each had suggested that the other resign from their positions and it really got nasty when each of them called on the other's Board of Directors to fire them.

Some college employees feared that the College Board of Directors might actually consider firing the President, so they decided to try to help him out. They created a petition supporting the college President and urging the Board to stand behind him. The petition would be presented to the Board at its monthly meeting the following week. Our college had two main campuses about twenty-five miles apart – one at 'Burg and one at 'Ville. The petition was first circulated at the 'Burg campus and many signatures were obtained.

The petition was then hand delivered to the 'Ville campus to be circulated for signatures. By now, time was short since the Board meeting was in three days, so several people worked almost full-time obtaining signatures from employees on the 'Ville campus.

The petition was going well and hundreds of signatures had been obtained. Word was around that the President was very pleased by the outpouring of support and was looking forward very much to having a half dozen employees, representing different employment groups of the college, make the presentation at the College Board meeting. That should shut up that school Superintendent who was hounding him.

It probably should be explained that not all of the employees liked or supported the college President. Not everyone supported the idea of creating the petition and presenting it to the Board and some people refused to sign the petition. It was also rumored that there was a little arm twisting going on to get people to sign the petition.

There was some back room discussion that when the President got his hands on the petition, analyzed the names on it and found that some were missing, there might be some retaliation.

Since some people were opposed to the petition and the presentation of it to the Board, the persons who were in charge of obtaining signatures guarded it carefully. They only hand delivered it to persons who were known to have the utmost loyalty to the President and who strongly supported the petition.

One of the business instructors from the 'Burg campus taught two classes on the 'Ville campus on Monday, Wednesday, and Friday. This instructor, Mary, was extremely loyal to the college President, had helped create the petition, and was to be one of the persons to present it to the College Board.

On Wednesday, the day before the College Board meeting, my colleague in the Business Department, John, and I were visiting in my office when a person carrying a 9" x 12" envelope entered our office complex looking for Mary.

"She's not here yet," John said, "but if that envelope is for her, you can just lay it on the desk that she uses right over there."

"Oh no," the courier said, "I'll stop back."

As soon as the courier left, John and I looked at each other knowingly and said almost in unison, "That was the petition."

It was clear that the obtaining of signatures on the 'Ville campus was completed and that the petition would now be hand delivered to the 'Burg campus by Mary for presentation to the Board at their meeting on that campus on Thursday night.

About fifteen minutes later, the bearer of the 9" x 12" envelope appeared again, looking for Mary. "She's not here yet," I said, "but if that envelope is for Mary, we'll give it to her if you want."

"No, no," the bearer of the envelope said, "I'll come back."

John and I looked at each other again, knowingly, and said in unison, "The petition."

It was apparent that the bearer of the envelope containing the petition did not consider John or me to be strong enough loyalists to be entrusted with the petition.

Here is a timetable that is of importance to this story:

Mary arrived at the 'Ville Business Department at approximately 10:40 a.m. on that Wednesday morning. I was in class and did not see her arrive. John was in the library and did not see her arrive, either.

At 11:00 a.m. John, Mary, and I all had classes, which ended at 11:50 a.m. Each of us arrived in the Business Department office around 11:55 a.m.

At around noon, John went to the college cafeteria for lunch. I grabbed a cup of coffee from the faculty lounge, returned to my office, and closed the door to work at my desk through the noon hour. Mary apparently worked at her desk for a while and then went to lunch around 12:45 p.m. Her office is out of sight from where I sit at my desk, so I cannot verify this precisely.

At some time that morning, the person with the 9" x 12" envelope apparently made contact with Mary.

Both John and I had classes starting at 1:00 p.m. and ending at 1:50 p.m. We both returned to the Business Department offices at approximately 1:55 p.m.

When I walked into the office, there was hysteria, pandemonium, and panic. There were a half dozen people in Mary's office, including Mary, sifting through everything on the desk, on the floor, everywhere.

"What's going on?" I asked

"The petition is missing," Mary said.

"What petition?" I asked.

"The *President's* petition," she moaned.

"Did you see anyone in Mary's office?" someone asked.

"I just got out of class," I said, "I had a one o'clock class."

"Me too," John said.

Since John and I had both been in class in front of thirty students, witnesses all, we were immediately eliminated as suspects.

The group searched Mary's office, books, briefcase, and even her clothes, but the petition was gone. Mary was certain that she had not misplaced it, so it was apparent that someone had stolen it. But how could they have done it without being seen? It was a mystery that would be discussed at Lakes Community College for many months.

The creators of the petition, those who gathered signatures, and those who signed it had looked forward to showing their support for the President. Now, with the Board of Directors' meeting just one day away, there would not be time to create another petition and to gather a sufficient number of signatures to make an impressive showing. And, presenting a half-baked petition would be worse than presenting no petition at all.

The petition had been a big, big deal for many of the college employees, and it was a huge deal for the college President. When it suddenly disappeared, word spread throughout the college like a raging wildfire.

"Who would have the audacity to steal the President's petition?" "Who would be dumb enough to risk their job to steal the President's petition?" "Who would have the balls to steal the petition?" "Why would someone steal it?" "Was it a traitor who supports the Superintendent that the President is feuding with?" "How did they steal it without being seen?" "Who will be the messenger to inform the President?"

The suspicions and questions went on and on. Everyone was dumbfounded that the petition had actually been stolen. For a small college that doesn't have too much excitement, it was comparable to the Great Brinks Robbery.

Rumors were rampant, and I must admit that I had a great deal of fun doing my best to fan the flames. "Maybe somebody who signed the petition under pressure stole it for spite." "Maybe someone who refused to sign it knew it would draw the fury of the President when he discovered their name missing." "Maybe the petition did not contain enough names to impress the Board and the originators of the petition ate it and blamed it on a thief." "Maybe the college President changed his mind and decided that he could handle that school Superintendent on his own without the help of the faculty and he ordered it quashed." "Maybe there was no petition."

In all the years that I taught, the missing petition was the hottest topic of conversation that ever occurred. It was talked about, speculated about, rumored about, and beat to death week after week.

By the way, the rift between the college President and the school Superintendent burned itself out and as it turned out, the President didn't need the support of the petition anyway.

Those of us in the Business Department, of course, were prime suspects in some people's minds, simply because we were located close to the scene of the crime.

My friend, John, and I had to continually remind people that each of us was in class from 1:00 p.m. to 1:50 p.m. This seemed to satisfy their suspicion and to get us off the hook.

You have probably heard the little saying about the word, *assume*. That is, if you assume something, it is possible you will make an ASS of U and ME.

In the case of the missing petition, it was widely *assumed* that the petition was taken sometime between 1:00 p.m. and when Mary discovered it missing at about 1:35 p.m. You might want to go back and review the timetable that I presented earlier in this story to see if that assumption appears to be correct.

You may have heard Paul Harvey's radio program, *The Rest of the Story*, where he revealed behind-the-scenes information about a well-known person or event. If you read on, to the following chapter of this book, and read very carefully, you will find *the Rest of the Story* about the missing petition.

Joining The Ranks

Two of my proudest days as a teacher were the day that the college Vice President asked me if I would have an interest in becoming an administrator (thus indicating that I was considered *worthy*), and the day that I turned down the offer to become an administrator (thus *proving* that I was worthy). They both happened on the same day.

Moonlighting

You might recall that my reason for choosing teaching as a career was that I perceived it to be a leisurely lifestyle where teachers had every weekend off, a month's vacation during the school year, and had three months off in the summer.

The one small factor that I had overlooked was that if you only work eight months of the year, you only get paid for eight months. This resulted in either living a modest lifestyle, or in finding ways to increase one's income by working nights, weekends, summers, and vacations, known as *moonlighting*. I desired a nice lifestyle for myself and for my family, and that took money, so I became what must have been one of the world's most active moonlighters.

In a quirky twist of fate, the work schedule back on the farm, that I became a teacher to avoid, would have been a leisurely existence compared to the schedule that I maintained during my thirty-eight years as a teacher. Here are some of the activities that I pursued in addition to being a full-time teacher.

Life Insurance Sales

By Thanksgiving of my first year of teaching, I figured out that my expectation of having a three-month summer vacation was only a pipe dream and that I would need to find a summer job.

One of my buddies from back home was selling life insurance and he told me about the great money that could be made from sales commissions. I studied for the state life insurance exam, passed it, and was ready to go when classes ended at the end of May.

A life insurance salesperson can earn a very good living if they average one or two sales per week. If they average three sales a week, they can live a fabulous lifestyle, and if they average more than three sales a week, they can live like a king.

I dove into my summertime job with a vengeance and made a sale my first day, and my second, and my third, and my fourth.

The insurance company had what they called "The Sixty Club," to which a salesperson would be admitted if they sold sixty policies in sixty consecutive days, including Saturdays and Sundays. Since most insurance salespeople sold maybe 10 to 18 policies in a sixty-day period, selling 60 was quite a feat and very few of the company's salespeople became members of the prestigious club. Far more rare was becoming a member in one's first sixty days on the job – it was almost unheard of.

Since I was off to a fast start, the general agent that I worked for started to push me to shoot for "The Sixty Club" in my first sixty days. I accepted the challenge and worked from about 8 a.m. to 9 or 10 p.m. Monday through Friday and put in seven or eight hours on Saturdays. I even made a sale on the Fourth of July.

By the end of my first sixty days as a life insurance salesman, I had made 63 sales.

My general agent talked to me about the great wealth that I could accumulate selling life insurance and almost begged me to break the teaching contract that I had signed for the following year and to continue with life insurance sales.

I was only twenty-two years old that summer and it is probably true that I would have been a millionaire by the time I was thirty had I stayed with life insurance sales. It is also true, I believe, that at the pace I was working, I would have been dead by age thirty-five.

I believed in what I was doing that summer that I sold life insurance, but I believed I could accomplish something much more worthwhile by continuing as a teacher. That is why I returned to teach my second year and why I never attempted to sell another life insurance policy after that summer.

Driver Training

When I was in college, someone advised me that if I was going to become a teacher, I should also obtain my driver training teacher certification, which I did.

When I got my first job as a high school teacher, I soon discovered that when someone got the summertime driver training job at the school, they held onto it for life. I could see why. All the driver-training teacher did was sit in the car all day listening to the radio while the student drivers drove them around town. Compared to roofing or painting, it was a cushy job.

I never expected to get a chance to teach driver training since the existing driver-training teacher at our school was so entrenched in the position. Then, unexpectedly, the school in a neighboring town needed a part-time driver-training teacher for the summer and I jumped at the chance.

Each driver training session with a new student driver started out the same – adjust the seat and the mirrors, fasten the seat belt, start the engine, turn on the turn signal, check for traffic, and slowly pull out onto the street.

Some of the student drivers had been driving on country back roads for years. They jumped in, rolled down the window, stuck out their elbow, started the engine, and tromped on the gas by the time I was halfway through the checklist. It was a constant battle to try to rein them in. Typically, they considered driving with two hands on the steering wheel to be for sissies and didn't' think it counted as real driving unless they kicked up some gravel or squealed the tires on takeoff.

The students were fourteen or fifteen years old and there were a few of them who were so short that they could not see over the steering wheel. Their entire visibility of the road was limited to that two-inch space where they could see out beneath the top of the steering wheel and above the dash. I'm sure that when we went down the road with one of those munchkins behind the wheel it appeared that it was a driverless car, which, actually, wasn't too far from the truth.

One student driver apparently had never steered anything in his life, such as a bicycle, tricycle, coaster wagon, or lawn mower. We bounced from the curb on one side of the street to the curb on the other side as he madly turned the steering wheel in one direction as fast as he could and then when we hit the curb, he'd madly turn the wheel all the way in the opposite direction.

I taught the students that before pulling out into an intersection from a stopped position they should always look left, then right, and then left again before proceeding.

One day one of the munchkins was driving when we stopped before the railroad tracks. The munchkin looked left – the train was coming. He looked right. He looked left again – the train was still coming. And then he pulled out. I slammed on my brake, which fortunately was installed on the passenger side of the car, and we came to a sliding stop sideways in the gravel road about six feet from the railroad tracks. Apparently I had forgot to tell the student that if, after looking left, right, left, something is coming, you should not pull out. How foolish of me not to mention it.

Most of the students were eager to get out of town and to do some highway driving. I would estimate that at least fifty percent of the time we took a curve two wheels remained on the pavement and the other two were on the shoulder kicking up gravel or mud.

The one thing that the students most looked forward to, especially the guys who had been driving since they were eight or nine years old, was the *Quick Stop*. This is where we would be driving along and suddenly I would yell, "STOP," as if some object had popped up in front of us on the road.

I always did the quick stop in town, since doing it out on the highway could be disastrous in at least a dozen different ways. There was only one street in town that was perfectly suited for the quick stop where there were no intersections for several blocks and where there was seldom any oncoming traffic.

Word got around and all of the students knew which street was used for the quick stop. In fact, it was a nightly ritual to measure the length of the day's skid marks. Apparently there was some contest going on.

When I told a student driver to pull onto the street where the quick stop would be executed, I could see their eyes light up. I tried to hold them down, but those guys who had been driving for a dozen years would not obey and by the time I yelled "STOP" we were sometimes going fifty or sixty miles an hour. That will lay a prize-winning patch of rubber any ol' day.

That was the only summer that I ever taught driver training. I never again put my name on any school's list as a possible substitute or replacement driver-training teacher. It was the most dangerous job that I ever had in my life and figured that I'd quit while I was ahead rather than tempt fate.

That one summer of teaching driver training changed my attitude towards those guys who taught driver training year after year. First of all, they had balls of steel. Second, I realized that the reason they looked so calm and serene sitting there in the passenger seat was that they were frozen with fear.

Two years after I retired from my stint as a driver-training teacher, one of the students rolled the driver training car. There, but by the grace of God, rolled I.

The Glass Man

My friend, Steve, and I taught at the same high school when we were both in our early twenties. Steve secured a job working part-time for the local glass company installing plate glass windows, household windows, and doing whatever else came along. The owner needed another part-time employee and Steve asked if I'd be interested, which is how I, too, became a *glass man*.

Steve and I often worked together on bigger jobs and usually everything went like clockwork. Occasionally, though, things went awry.

I recall the time that the boss sent Steve and me to the bus depot to replace the large plate glass window that was broken. When we got there, we found that the bottom right-hand corner of the window was cracked and was held together with duct tape. We carefully removed the frame holding the window, removed the window, and loaded it on the truck.

We measured carefully and set about cutting to size the large piece of glass that we had brought along. Steve scored the piece of glass with the glasscutter; it looked like a good score. The final step was to clamp onto the edge of the glass where the score had been made with a special pair of pliers. With a quick snap of the wrist, the glass would break off cleanly where the score had been made. At least, that's the theory. This time, however, it didn't go as planned and a piece about eight inches high and six inches wide broke off of the bottom left-hand corner.

When we had arrived at the bus depot, the bottom

right-hand corner of the window was broken and was taped together with duct tape. When we left the bus depot, there was a new piece of glass in its place, with the bottom left-hand corner broken and taped together with duct tape. I never heard if they ever got that window replaced.

Another time, the boss sent me to replace a door closure on an aluminum door leading to an upstairs apartment above a retail store. A door closure is that gizmo at the top of a large door that allows it to close smoothly with a whoosh sound rather than slamming shut.

I removed the old door closure and held the brand new one up in place. The holes from the new one didn't match the holes from the old one, so I marked four new holes on the door for the closure and marked two new holes on the doorframe for the arm of the closure. I drilled the new holes and bolted the new door closure in place. It didn't work.

I examined the door and the door closure and discovered the problem. I moved the closure over a couple of inches and drilled some new holes. I bolted the closure in place, but again it didn't work.

I took a little walk down the street, nonchalantly observing how door closures were supposed to be attached to the door and finally figured out where I had gone wrong, maybe.

I repositioned the door closure and drilled some more holes. This time it worked. When I got done, the aluminum door looked worse than the car that Bonnie and Clyde were riding in when they were ambushed – I had drilled eighteen new holes in the door and the frame, in addition to the six that were there in the beginning.

Thank God for aluminum caulking. I filled the holes as best I could and smoothed them over with a putty knife. If I must say so myself, the door looked pretty good when I left. Not great, maybe, but pretty good.

IGL Recording Company

When I was a teenager in the late 1950's and early 1960's radio stations played a blend of Rock 'N Roll and Country music and I came to love both styles.

I started writing songs when I was in my mid twenties and hounded every musician and band within a hundred miles, begging them to listen to a tape of my songs in the hope that they might want to record it. This led me to IGL Recording Company, which was one of the first professional recording studios in the state and which was located only about twenty-five miles from where I lived.

IGL Recording Company was a booming operation in those days because it had recorded a national hit record a few years before and bands from several states around came to IGL to try to capture that same magic.

The recording studio was owned by four guys and when one of them wanted out so he could devote more time to his radio and television business, the other guys asked me if I wanted to buy his share, which I did.

IGL was a custom recording studio, which meant that the bands had to pay to record in the studio. I was the

Promotions Director and was responsible for helping the bands gain publicity for their record releases. I also recruited bands to come record there and produced a number of albums for groups.

I was actively involved with IGL Recording Company for about eight years before other interests started to occupy my time. It was one of the most exciting activities I have ever been involved in. We recorded numerous albums and records, but never had another national hit record after I became a partner. Hmmmm.

I have sometimes wondered what my high school band director, rest his soul, who deservedly gave me an "F" in band, would have thought if he knew that I ended up writing songs, owning a professional recording studio, and being inducted into the state's Rock 'N' Roll Hall of Fame. I think he would have been very pleased and I think he would have grinned from ear to ear.

Real Estate Sales

On my way to work at Lakes Community College I often stopped at this wonderful bakery to pick up a roll or two to serve as my breakfast or mid-morning snack. About three times a week I met this same guy on the sidewalk as I was heading into the bakery and he was heading to his office down the block. For the first month or so we just greeted each other with a friendly "Hello." As time passed over the next year, our greetings evolved into, "Nice day," "How are you," "Have a nice day," "Have a good weekend," "Good seeing you again," and so on.

One Saturday night my wife and I were in a restaurant when I spied this guy a few tables away. "There he is;" I told my wife, "there's the guy that I see two or three times a week when I stop at the bakery."

At about the same time, he spotted me and was apparently telling his wife the same thing about me. Then he rose and approached us and said, "Hi, I'm Ken. I see you so often that I feel like I know you."

Ken and his wife, Jean, joined us and we had a wonderful time and got along fabulously. Ken sold real estate. I mentioned that I had thought about selling real estate part-time some day and he suggested that I get myself licensed and join him as a partner.

I received my real estate license a few months later and prepared to join him selling real estate. I planned to keep my teaching position at the College and to sell real estate evenings and weekends. If I had real estate matters that needed attention during a weekday, Ken would handle it. Likewise, I would cover for Ken evenings and weekends.

Ken was excited about my joining him in the real estate business and wanted to make an announcement in the local newspaper. I did not want to irritate the administration at the College, so I asked my boss if it was okay. He said it was. Wanting to cover my backside a little more thoroughly, I also asked my boss's boss and he, too, said it was okay to make the announcement.

I knew my new friend, Ken, pretty well by that time, but

I didn't know exactly how he operated, which I soon found out is *full throttle ahead*. Ken ran a full-page ad in the newspaper every day for a week and a half with a picture of me at least a foot tall announcing that I was joining him in the real estate business. I had people stop me on the street and say that they were going to cancel their subscription to the newspaper if they saw my picture one more time. They were just kidding, maybe.

About the time that the full-page ad had run for about a week, my colleague in the Business Department, John, and I were taking a shortcut from our office to the faculty lounge by going through the auditorium. The college President was arranging some chairs and tables in preparation for that night's Board of Directors meeting.

"Say, Pete," he said to me, "what's your telephone extension here at the college?"

"Extension 168," I replied.

"Then why in the hell don't you put that in the newspaper too," he snarled. And then he grabbed a stack of papers and threw them down on one of the tables in disgust and stomped off muttering to himself, leaving John and me standing there, dumbfounded.

"I'll get that son-of-a-bitch for you some day," John said.

Around a year later, at precisely 12:54 p.m. on a Wednesday, John fulfilled his pledge, with me as his able assistant.

Ken and I were very successful in our real estate partnership. I worked the business about 30 hours a week evenings and weekends and Ken worked the business weekdays. We dissolved the partnership after about four years when Ken got a chance to buy into a large real estate and insurance office and I was offered a contract to write a book for a major publisher. It was perfect timing for both of us. Ken remains one of the best friends that I've ever had and we are in regular contact.

After that incident with the college President in the auditorium, he totally ignored me for the next two or three years. If I was in a group of four people, he might bring a cup of coffee for the other three, but not for me. If there were three of us in a group and he introduced us to a visitor on campus, he skipped over me like I didn't exist. Fortunately, I only saw him face-to-face a few times a year, and I learned how to stay out of his way.

Intimidation was the President's favorite tool for putting people in their place. He once got mad at his personal secretary and had her sit at her desk every day for over a month without talking to her and without giving her any work to do.

The great friendship that I developed with Ken and the success that we experienced in the real estate business far outweighed the small amount of abuse that I suffered at the hands of the college President. And, that little incident in the auditorium triggered one of the greatest capers that I was ever involved in as a teacher.

Real Estate Pre-License Course

I loved being in real estate sales and I love the real estate industry. After I quit selling real estate to devote my time to writing books, I was asked if I would teach the state Real Estate Pre-License Course in our area and I agreed. The course was mandatory before a person could sit for the state real estate exam, so there were always enough students to fill a class every semester. It was a sixty-hour course that met one night a week for four hours for fifteen consecutive weeks.

A few years later I was asked if I would teach the Pre-License course on television, and it was broadcast to about one-fourth of the state.

Students in the Pre-License course were highly interested adults who paid hundreds of dollars of their own money for the course and many of them were knowledgeable bankers, insurance salespeople, teachers, and business operators. It was the most demanding course that I ever taught, but it was also one of the most interesting and rewarding.

I taught the state Real Estate Pre-License course thirty-four times over seventeen years and estimate that I trained about 750 Realtors. I know that I will have to answer for this on *Judgment Day*.

The Author

As a youth, I always had a paperback in my back pocket and would read every chance I got. I loved Zane Grey westerns and Sherlock Holmes mysteries.

When I was nineteen years old, a combination of receiving a few nice comments on some of my college term papers and getting some compliments from a few college friends about letters I wrote them in the summertime, spawned the idea that I wanted to be a writer.

I started teaching in high school at age twenty-one and, in addition to teaching, was extremely busy for the next four years studying for my Master's degree and working at various part-time jobs to survive. I finally had some time to pursue my interest in writing when I took a teaching position at Lakes Community College.

I wrote a couple of books that were published by smaller publishers when I was in my twenties. I wrote some other manuscripts that are in my basement in a box with a label that says, *MANUSCRIPTS THAT WERE NOT PUBLISHED, AND NEVER WILL BE.*

Shoebox Accounting

My friend and neighbor, Ron, was a CPA who operated his own accounting office. One summer morning he called and said that he was going out of town to see his client, Biff, and he asked me to ride along so we could visit a little bit. As you know, accountants are tight-lipped and he didn't say anything more than we were going to visit his client, Biff, and I didn't ask him because I figured he wouldn't tell me anyway.

We headed down the highway, turned off onto a blacktop, and eventually came to this small town and parked in front of Biff's Tavern at about 9 a.m. Biff's wasn't open for business, but the door was open for my friend's arrival. We walked inside and a guy with shaggy hair and a beard came running from the back of the place and yelled, "Do you think

I'm going to jail?"

"Man, this is going to be fun," I thought to myself. And it was.

As it turned out, Biff had every good reason to ask if he was headed for jail since he had not filed income taxes for five or six years. We carried boxes and bags of Biff's chaotic financial records out of his office and put them in Ron's car for him to take back to his accounting office to sort through and make some sense of. An accounting system like Biff's has been referred to by accountants for years and years as a *Shoebox Accounting System*. It's where a person's financial records are just haphazardly thrown into a shoebox, or in Biff's case, boxes and bags, with the intention of straightening them out later, which rarely comes.

The thought occurred to me at that moment, "What a great way this would be to create a college accounting student simulation, where everything is there, but is purposefully in a state of disarray, just like Biff's stuff."

I wrote that simulation, called *Skeeter's Pizza Parlor – The Shoebox Accounting Practice Set*, and presented it to the accounting editor at McGraw-Hill Book Company of New York, one of the world's great publishers. Normally, a writer suffers through rejection after rejection before finding a publisher, if at all, but with The Shoebox, the first publisher I submitted it to accepted it for publication. It was the first of its kind ever published in the world and was been on the market for over twenty-five years.

In obtaining my Bachelor's and Master's degrees in

business, I took six or seven accounting courses, which means that I know enough about accounting only to be dangerous. There are literally millions of *real* accountants out there who know so much more about accounting than I do and who undoubtedly are familiar with the concept of *shoebox accounting*. Therefore, through the years, I have marveled at how I was the lucky one to come up with the idea for the Shoebox Accounting Practice Set instead of one of those real accountants. I believe the answer is, simply, that I went to Biff's Tavern that day and they didn't. I listed my friend, Ron, on the cover of *The Shoebox Accounting Practice Set* as a consultant as a tip of the hat for taking me to Biff's that day.

Writing Up A Storm

The accounting editor at McGraw-Hill loved *The Shoebox Accounting Practice Set* and she loved me. When her colleague, the business mathematics editor, was seeking an author for a new textbook, she recommended me. I wrote or co-wrote three business math textbooks for McGraw-Hill. The business math editor and I became close friends and when I told her that I had just finished writing a non-fiction book manuscript, *Earn Money at Home*, she got me in touch with an editor in the general book division. I wrote several non-fiction books for the bookstore market for that editor. Networking.

I have been a serious writer for over thirty-five years now and have written twenty-five books that have been published including college textbooks, fiction and nonfiction books for the bookstore market, children's picture books, and this one. I have also added a few manuscripts to that box in my basement over the years.

Ideas for books come from everywhere and you never know when someone will make an offhand comment or you'll see something that triggers your imagination. One book idea came from an unlikely source. The President of the College who got so mad at me when I entered the real estate business part-time continued through the years to be upset with teachers who, in his mind, overly pursued part-time jobs or had second careers. He once made a speech to the faculty saying something like, "This moonlighting is getting out of hand – there's teachers selling real estate, doing landscaping, operating truck gardens, working in retail stores, selling things – moonlighting, moonlighting, moonlighting."

I thought to myself, "What a great idea for a book." A couple of years later, my book, *MOONLIGHTING – A Complete Guide To Over 200 Exciting Part-Time Jobs*, was published by McGraw-Hill Book Company in both hardcover and paperback and was sold in bookstores across America. Thanks, Mr. President.

The Shoebox Accounting Practice Set was considered to be a creative idea by the editors at McGraw-Hill, but it probably was not my most creative idea for a book.

Many years ago, I got the idea that virtually all of the non-fiction books on the market were written in a straightforward style that was informative but boring to read. What I thought would be a better approach was a series of books, on virtually any and all topics, that presented good, solid, useful information in an upbeat and even mildly humorous way. I prepared a proposal and wrote the first sixty pages of a book in this style called *The Nitwit's Guide to Investing*.

I presented my idea to a top literary agent from New York that I was working with at the time and she said, "Oh, my gosh – we can't call people nitwits. No publisher in the world would ever publish anything like this. It's a bad idea." I assumed that the literary agent knew what she was talking about and I dropped the idea.

This was, by the way, more than a decade before the *Dummies* books hit the market. I still have nightmares of a train loaded with money going past my house and not stopping – a trainload that should have been mine. That literary agent and I no longer speak.

I spent tens of thousands of hours writing over the years. Since I was teaching full-time and pursued some of the other activities that I have described in this chapter at the same time, I often wrote in my home office until midnight three or four nights a week and often spent entire weekends writing as well. Like I said, when I was nineteen years old, I decided that I wanted to be a writer.

Meet Peter Davidson

My name is David Peterson. In virtually every town I have lived, there were one, two, or maybe even three other guys named David Peterson. I would often get their bills or other mail by mistake and they would often get mine. When we got mail intended for one of the other David Petersons, we would simply write, "Sorry, opened by mistake," on the envelope, tape it back together, and give it to the post office to route to the correct David Peterson.

One day, I received a love letter intended for another David Peterson by mistake. Then, I opened it by mistake, and then I read it by mistake, four times. Actually, it was the first perfumed letter I had received in many years, so I ripped it open. The letter started out, "Dear Dave, Last night when we were . . . .," well, you can use your imagination. Think as steamy as you can and then multiply that by ten and you're in the ballpark.

This presented me with a predicament. I figured that if I taped the envelope back together and wrote on it, "Sorry, opened by mistake," they would know that human eyes had read this very, very private, and steamy, letter – and had probably made photocopies of it. I decided that the only decent and humane thing to do was to keep the letter and to let them believe forever that the letter had gotten lost in the mail system or had simply disintegrated because of spontaneous combustion.

I wish I had been there, though, when she said to him, "Dave, did you get my letter?" and he replied, "What letter?"

All I can say is, "Dave, you're a lucky dog."

I still have the letter, by the way, and I still read it about once a month for inspiration.

Oh, here's where this story is supposed to be going. Since I came to think of my name, David Peterson, as such a common and ordinary name and I wanted something a little more distinctive for my writings, I shifted the syllables around and came up with the pen name, Peter Davidson. That's me.

The college textbooks that I wrote are under my real name, David Peterson, the non-fiction books and novels are under my pen name, Peter Davidson, and, as you might have noticed, this book was written by both of us.

Peter Davidson's Writer's Seminars

One thing often leads to another. The publishing success that I achieved gave me the idea that it would be fun to present writer's seminars for persons interested in writing books, magazine articles, short stories, poetry, and other works for possible publication. I created *Peter Davidson's Writer's Seminar,* put together about forty pages of handouts, and booked the seminar through the Continuing Education offices of several community colleges in the state. I didn't know what to expect – would anyone be interested? Would anyone show up?

More than fifty people showed up for that first writer's seminar and they have continued to show up year after year since then at over 635 one-day seminars that I have presented in fifteen states over a twenty-five year period.

When I was teaching full-time, I usually booked seminars for ten straight Saturdays in the fall and booked eight seminars on Saturdays in the winter. I had six weeks' vacation in the summer, and I booked a four- or five-week seminar tour through five or six states. My wife and I packed up our SUV and away we went. We were like a rock band out on tour, except we couldn't sing.

I love writing, whether it is books, songs, short stories, or anonymous Poison Pen memos to the faculty. It is a lonely business, though, where I sit in a room all alone with the door closed and mumble to myself. The writer's seminars were something that my wife and I did together – I spoke and she took care of registering the participants and sold writer's reference books during the breaks and noon hour. It was a nice change of pace for a writer, we had a great time on our travels, the seminars were tremendously successful, and we were treated like royalty wherever we presented a seminar.

We have many "Stories from the Road," but that's another book. But, let me tell you one. I was standing outside the building at a community college in Colorado, grabbing a last bit of solitude before beginning my seminar presentation when a guy with long hair, a big beard, sunglasses, and leather clothing pulled up on a loud motorcycle and asked, "Hey, buddy, where's that Harley Davidson's Rider's Seminar?"

All Work And No Play…

An old saying states, more or less, "All work and no play makes you a dull person." It might appear that I was a workaholic during my thirty-eight year teaching career what with all of the moonlighting activities and additional careers that I was involved in – and I didn't list everything here. By my calculations, when I add up the number of years that I was involved in my various moonlighting activities, I worked the equivalent of 119 years during that 38-year period.

But, I did not work all the time. My wife and I had an active social life and we went out at least three nights per week, and we still do. Besides, many of my moonlighting activities, like the recording studio, writing books, and presenting seminars, fall more into the category of fun than work, at least for me.

I read somewhere that the average adult watches something like twenty-eight hours of television per week. When I was at my busiest, I would watch maybe one hour of television a month and I once went six months without seeing any television programs at all. I never saw some of the popular television shows of the day and some people have told me I didn't miss much. I simply was having more fun creating works of my own than watching something that someone else had created.

Surviving

I did not survive as a teacher for thirty-eight years by accident. I survived partly because of luck, partly because of the wonderful colleagues that I worked with, partly because I didn't get caught at various things that might have gotten me fired, and partly because of various strategies that I developed and followed through the years.

Over the past several decades, many books have been written on how to be successful on the job or in your career. Many of the books contain wonderful theories but, when put into practice, they don't actually work for people in the trenches. Forget those books. Following is the real stuff. I created these survival techniques specifically for teachers, but they can be applied by anyone in any profession, career, or job. They sure worked for me.

Survival Techniques

- If it appears that you're going to have to do it anyway, try to make it look like it was your idea in the first place.
- If it appears that you're going to have to do it anyway, do it with a smile on your face - it will thoroughly piss off your boss.
- If it appears that you're going to have to do it anyway, volunteer – it will so confound and confuse your boss

that they'll think that you're up to something and they'll never ask you to do it again.
- If a problem confronts you that you must discuss with your boss, <u>always</u> present the problem <u>and</u> your proposed solution to your boss at the same time. As you know, your boss isn't the brightest bulb on the tree and if you leave it up to them to create a solution, it will result in utter chaos.
- Respect the office secretaries and cultivate a strong working relationship and friendship with them. They are, after all, the ones who make the school run. If they like you, they can, and will, do little favors for you that will make your life much easier. If they don't like you, they can make your life a living hell.
- Respect the custodians and cultivate a strong working relationship and friendship with them. Besides their being able to do little favors for you, there is another good reason to form this bond.

In some strange quirk of human behavior, school administrators often form stronger personal friendships with the custodians than with the faculty. Maybe it's because the administrators, too, have figured out that the custodians can do little favors for them and make their life easier. Most likely, though, the reason is probably that the custodians don't pose a threat to them whereas the faculty is always lurking around the corner waiting for them to make a mistake so they can hang their ass. And, if the custodian puts in a good word for

you with the boss, it will carry more weight than a letter of recommendation from the Governor.
- When you walk, always carry something in your hand – it makes it look like you're going somewhere on a mission.
- It seems that education is the last thing that school administrators want to chitchat about. Find their hot button whether it is a professional football team they love, a personal hobby, or a special interest, and ask them about that when you bump into them in the hallway. They'll light up like a candle and they will think you're great – and a great teacher.
- If you discover a school-wide problem that needs to be addressed or a procedure that needs to be changed, DO NOT point it out to the administration – it is the fastest way on earth to volunteer to head up the committee to study the problem or situation. Instead, mention the problem at a Faculty Association meeting and, if the membership agrees with your contention, have the Association forward the concern to the administration. That way, it will come from the group and you will not be singled out.
- It is unavoidable that occasionally there will be touchy-feely in-service sessions where some so-called expert from a thousand miles away will get everyone into groups of six or eight to discuss some harebrained topic. One of their favorites, I found, is, "Reveal your worst personal trait and discuss it with the group." Some in the group will take this seriously and will confess, "I cheat on my

income taxes," "I drink 60-70 bottles of beer a week," "I'm afraid of the dark," "I'm impotent," "I have sexual desires for my students of the opposite sex," or "I still wet the bed at night."

Don't be stupid. The rest of them in your group are taking mental notes and will spread your secret all over town. Instead, say something that sounds like a weakness but that, upon closer inspection, is actually a strength. Say something like, "I work too hard at my teaching job for my own good, putting in 70 or 80 hours a week," "I take my students' failures personally and lie awake nights trying to figure out how to better inspire them to learn," or "I am on the verge of having financial problems because I donate too much money to the church." If they want to find out about the junk in your trunk, make them beat it out of you.

- Do not volunteer for anything. It will only make you vulnerable to criticism and subject to punishment if that for which you volunteered flops. And, if that for which you volunteered becomes a huge success, somebody else, somewhere, will take the credit for it anyway.
- Do not volunteer for anything. It will only earn you a reputation as a *volunteerer* or as an eager beaver who wants to "get involved" and you'll soon be on every committee that comes along.
- Be aware of the silent but powerful messages sent by your body language. When attending a meeting where you might be observed by your boss, always sit up

straight and place your feet flat on the floor parallel to each other. If you must rest your head in your hand to keep it from crashing to the table or desk, curl your little finger and ring finger as to make a fist, place your index finger alongside of your face, place your middle finger in front of your chin and your thumb beneath your chin. You will look wistful, contemplative, scholarly, and interested, and it will hold your head up. Practice this in the mirror until you have perfected the position.

Occasionally, write something in a notebook or on a full-sized sheet of paper; it will appear that you have recognized the speaker's vast wisdom and are interested enough in the goings on to take notes, even if in reality you're writing a letter to a friend or are writing over and over, "I hate this damn meeting."

- Keep all of your old reports, committee notes, and completed forms. When a new administrator comes on board, they will undoubtedly feel compelled to change things, even though everything is working flawlessly as it is. And, most likely, they'll change things back to the way they were before the previous administrator changed everything.
- Your file cabinet can be your best friend. If the subject matter stays the same from year to year, such as history or math, and if there's a different bunch of students in the class from year to year or semester to semester, use the same stuff.
- Remember that 76.859% of the statistics quoted in an

argument or debate are fabricated on the spot, including this one. Use this technique to your profound advantage.
- When working in a group, wear bright colors and move your arms a lot.
- Learn which things are traceable and which things are not. For instance, making personal long distance phone calls from your office phone that are billed to the school can get you fired. With other stuff, there's no way of knowing who did what, when, where, or why.
- If you must write that scorching memo to an administrator, use your head – don't sign it.
- Always turn in required reports on their exact due date. Turning them in ahead of time may give the impression that you have so little to do that you can easily whip up a report with time to spare. Turning them in late may draw the ire of the recipient of the report and it singles you out as someone who can't or won't follow the rules, who is lazy or defiant, or who can't handle the job.
- When completing that annual evaluation of your boss, be as positive as possible in the written evaluation. If you have negative things to say, discuss them verbally with the boss in person. You will get your point across, but the boss won't consider you to be a traitor for ratting on them to their boss. You can always do that later, if you need to.
- If you feel compelled to tell a colleague some inside information or juicy gossip and are fearful that you might get in trouble if it is learned that you said what

you are about to say, always preface your message with these words, "If you quote me, I'll deny it."

- If you know you're going to be tied up in a lengthy worthless meeting, plan in advance to have a secretary or colleague summon you from the meeting at some pre-arranged time – like fifteen minutes into the meeting. It will appear to everyone that there is important business at hand that you and only you can handle, thus elevating your stature within the group. And, once you're out of there, don't go back unless it's for the final ten minutes of the session.
- You will be required to attend many mindless gatherings, receptions, or activities or may feel compelled to do so to stay in the good graces of the administration. And, your being there or not being there will not affect the activity or its outcome in any way, since you are only a face in the crowd. And, some of these events will drag on for hours and hours, wasting your precious time that could be spent better down at Shooter's Pub or taking a good nap. So, be there, but don't be there.

Dress in your finest and arrive at the event fifteen or twenty minutes early. Make a mental list of people that need to see you there and circulate until each of them have talked to you once or have seen you walk past twice. Then, when the event officially begins, slip out the back door. As an example - at this very moment that I am sitting here in my office writing these words, I am supposed to be at a graduation ceremony, and I am. Over a hundred people would swear that they saw me and that I am there. I would explain further, but my wife and my friends, Al and Linda, are waiting for me down at Shooter's.

- Face it. In a school bureaucracy you're not going to make a difference in the way things work. Do your job, keep a low profile, and stay out of the way.

The Decision

I was twenty-one years old when I started teaching in high school and could have easily passed for one of the students.

I was twenty-five years old when I started teaching at Lakes Community College and, occasionally, one of the pretty college girls would say to me, "You remind me of my brother." What a cool thing to say.

As time passed, some of the college girls said to me, "You remind me of my dad," which was a nice compliment, I suppose.

When the college girls started saying to me, "You remind me of my grandpa," it was time for me to start thinking of hitting the road.

On The Road To Recovery

A few days before I handed in my resignation that would end my teaching career after thirty-eight years, I reflected on how quickly those years had passed. I was proud of the job that I had done and of the lives that I had touched positively. I was grateful that I had chosen and stayed in a career where I had the opportunity to make a worthwhile contribution to society. I was thankful that I had enjoyed the good health and stamina that allowed me to fulfill my obligations as a teacher and to pursue numerous other activities as well. I was relieved that I made it through all those years without getting fired and without being involved in a scandal. And I had a good time; in fact, I had a great time.

I was fortunate to work with dedicated and professional colleagues in the teaching ranks and to have the friendship, assistance, and support of the secretaries, custodians, and others who help a school run smoothly.

Even though in this book I poked fun at some of the administrators that I worked with and told some stories about their shortcomings, I actually got along with them very well, except for an incident or two. Since I probably worked with at least forty administrators, not all of my stories included in this book are about the same person.

The college President who got so mad at me over selling

real estate part-time eventually came to like me and he twice selected me to represent the college at a national community college conference in Austin, Texas. I was also selected as the "Teacher of the Year" twice at Lakes Community College, which didn't happen without his approval. The President and I exchanged Christmas cards for a dozen years after he retired. Whoda thunk it?

I chose the teaching profession because I perceived that it was a leisurely lifestyle. On my first week on the job I discovered that this was not true. Even though there were other opportunities outside of education that I could have pursued, I never seriously considered leaving the teaching profession. Why? Because I was a *teacher* and a teacher should teach.

I tried to leave no unfinished business behind me when I packed up my stuff and headed towards home for the last time.

As one of my final acts, I wrote the following memo and presented it to the office secretaries:

TO: Office Secretaries
FROM: Dave Peterson

Doesn't it just bug you when there is a nagging question that you don't know the answer to, when there is a riddle that you can't solve, when someone is playing a little trick on you, or when someone tells you that they have a secret but they won't tell you what it is.

That is why I thought you would like to know that when I leave the building for the last time this afternoon,
(OVER)

(Note – The rest of the message was on the backside of the sheet, with the capitalized word handwritten in big red letters.)

ELVIS, too, will have left the building.